SPAIN AND PORTUGAL TRAVEL GUIDE 2025

A Journey Through Culture, Cuisine, and Captivating Landscapes

John R. Hendrix

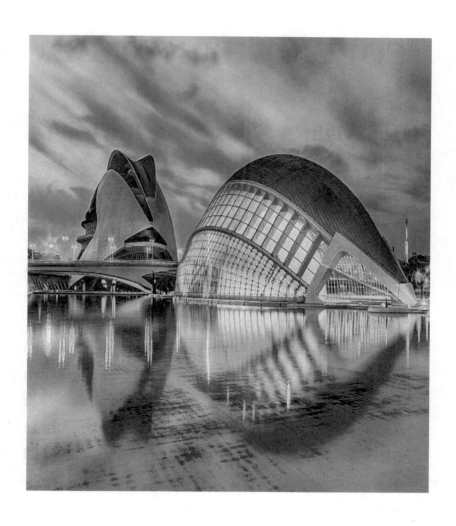

COPYRIGHT NOTICE

TABLE OF CONTENT

SCAN WITH DEVICE TO VIEW MAP

FOLLOW THE BELOW STEPS TO SCAN THE ABOVE QR CODE

How to Use Your Spain and Portugal Map QR Code:

❖ **Open your phone's camera app.**
❖ **Point the camera at the QR code** in your Spain and Portugal travel guide. Make sure the code is fully visible and centered in the camera's viewfinder.
❖ **Wait for your phone to recognize the code.** A notification will appear on your screen with a link to an interactive map of Spain and Portugal .
❖ **Tap the notification** to open the map. You can now explore Spain and Portugal stunning landscapes and plan your itinerary!

Note: If your phone doesn't automatically recognize QR codes, you might need to download a QR code reader app from your app store.

 SCAN ME

MY EXPERIENCE IN SPAIN AND PORTUGAL

As I embarked on my journey through Spain and Portugal, I had no idea how deeply these two countries would capture my heart. From the moment I arrived, it felt like stepping into a dream—a blend of ancient history, modern vibrancy, and landscapes that took my breath away at every turn.

My first stop was Madrid, where the grandeur of the Royal Palace and the cultural wealth of the Prado Museum immediately overwhelmed me. But it wasn't just the landmarks that left a mark—it was the charming, hidden alleyways lined with vibrant street art, the energy of the local markets, and the conversations with locals that made me feel like I was discovering the real soul of Spain. At night, I found myself seated at a cozy corner in a traditional tapas bar, savoring jamón ibérico and sipping a glass of Rioja, while the lively hum of laughter and conversation filled the air.

From Madrid, my journey took me to Barcelona, where I found myself lost in the surreal world of

Antoni Gaudí's masterpieces. La Sagrada Familia was even more awe-inspiring in person than I had imagined, with its intricate spires reaching toward the sky, as though it was alive. Strolling through Park Güell felt like walking through a fairy tale, with colorful mosaics and imaginative structures unfolding before me. But what surprised me most about Barcelona was the blend of old and new—the ancient Gothic Quarter contrasted beautifully with the modern vibe of the city's beach-lined coast.

Seville was pure magic, with its orange-scented streets and the sound of flamenco echoing through the air. I wandered through the Alcázar, captivated by the Moorish architecture and lush gardens. And then, as evening fell, I found myself seated in a small flamenco bar, watching as the dancers' passionate movements told stories older than time. The rhythm, the emotion—it was as if the spirit of Seville was dancing with them.

In Portugal, I found a different kind of charm. Lisbon, with its seven hills and endless miradouros, offered sweeping views of the city and the shimmering Tagus River. I spent hours wandering through Alfama, the city's oldest district, getting lost in its narrow, winding streets while Fado music drifted from nearby cafes.

The soulful tunes seemed to perfectly match the melancholic beauty of the city, and I could feel the deep connection the Portuguese people have to their history and culture.

Porto, with its medieval charm and iconic bridges, was equally enchanting. I'll never forget the afternoon spent in the Ribeira district, watching the sun set over the Douro River while sipping a glass of port wine. It was here, in Porto's historic streets, that I felt time slow down, allowing me to simply enjoy the moment—the sights, the sounds, the flavors.

My exploration didn't end with the cities. From the beaches of the Algarve, where golden cliffs met turquoise waters, to the rolling vineyards of the Douro Valley, the natural beauty of these countries was beyond anything I had imagined. The Benagil Caves in Portugal, in particular, left me speechless. The way the sunlight filtered through the cave's open ceiling and danced on the ocean below was nothing short of magical.

Spain and Portugal offered me not just a travel experience, but a journey of discovery. These countries, with their rich histories, warm people, and breathtaking landscapes, became more than just destinations—they became places that will forever hold a piece of my heart. And as I boarded my flight home, I knew that I wasn't saying goodbye, but rather, "see you again."

INTRODUCTION

Why Spain and Portugal?

Spain and Portugal are two of Europe's most fascinating destinations, offering an incredible blend of history, culture, natural beauty, and modern amenities. Whether you're a history buff, a foodie, an adventurer, or simply looking to relax on sun-soaked beaches, these Iberian neighbors provide something for every type of traveler.

Both countries have a rich cultural heritage that dates back thousands of years, marked by influences from the Romans, Moors, and other civilizations. Spain is famous for its vibrant cities like Barcelona, Madrid, and Seville, where architectural masterpieces, such as Gaudí's creations or Moorish palaces, blend seamlessly with modern urban life. Meanwhile, Portugal offers a more laid-back experience, from the picturesque, cobbled streets of Lisbon and Porto to the stunning landscapes of the Douro Valley and the dramatic coastlines of the Algarve.

One of the main reasons to visit Spain and Portugal is the diversity of experiences they offer within relatively short distances. In Spain, you can go from hiking the Pyrenees to exploring medieval castles or enjoying the Mediterranean beaches, all within a few hours. In Portugal, you can sip world-renowned port wine in Porto, stroll through Lisbon's historic Alfama district, or take a boat tour along the volcanic shores of the Azores.

The gastronomic appeal of Spain and Portugal is undeniable. Spain's tapas culture, famed paella, and jamón ibérico are culinary highlights, while Portugal is known for its seafood, especially bacalhau (salted cod), and its sweet pastéis de nata (custard tarts). Both countries are also home to famous wine regions—Spain's La Rioja and Portugal's Douro Valley being two of the most iconic.

Lastly, the warm hospitality and relaxed lifestyle of the locals make visitors feel welcome, whether you're sipping a café con leche at a bustling Spanish café or enjoying a Fado performance in a quaint Portuguese tavern. With a deep sense of tradition combined with modern comforts, Spain and Portugal are ideal destinations for travelers looking for a rich and rewarding travel experience.

Quick Facts About Spain and Portugal

Spain:

- **Capital**: Madrid
- **Population**: Approximately 47 million

- **Official Language**: Spanish (Castilian); regional languages include Catalan, Basque, and Galician.
- **Currency**: Euro (€)
- **Time Zone**: Central European Time (CET)
- **Major Cities**: Madrid, Barcelona, Seville, Valencia, Granada
- **Famous For**: Flamenco, tapas, bullfighting, festivals like La Tomatina and Feria de Abril, historic cities, world-class art museums (Prado Museum, Guggenheim Bilbao), La Sagrada Familia.
- **Geography**: Spain covers diverse terrains, from the beaches of Costa del Sol and Costa Brava to the mountains of the Pyrenees and the vast plains of Castilla.
- **Climate**: Mediterranean in coastal regions, with hot summers and mild winters; continental climate in central regions with more extreme temperatures.

Portugal:

- **Capital**: Lisbon
- **Population**: Approximately 10 million
- **Official Language**: Portuguese
- **Currency**: Euro (€)

- **Time Zone**: Western European Time (WET)
- **Major Cities**: Lisbon, Porto, Faro, Coimbra
- **Famous For**: Fado music, port wine, Azulejos (decorative tiles), seafood, explorers like Vasco da Gama, beautiful beaches, and the historic cities of Lisbon and Porto.
- **Geography**: Portugal is characterized by rolling hills, rugged coastlines, and the lush valleys of the Douro and Alentejo regions. It also includes two autonomous archipelagos: Madeira and the Azores.
- **Climate**: Mediterranean in most regions, with warm summers and mild winters; maritime climate in coastal areas and more temperate conditions in the islands.

How to Use This Guide

This travel guide is designed to help you make the most of your visit to Spain and Portugal by providing a comprehensive resource filled with essential travel information, insider tips, and cultural insights. Whether you're planning a two-week vacation or a weekend getaway, this guide will equip you with the knowledge to enjoy a smooth and enriching journey.

Here's how you can navigate through the guide:

1. **Planning Your Trip**: Start here if you're still in the early stages of planning your adventure. This section includes advice on when to visit, transportation options, visa and passport requirements, and tips for budgeting your trip. It's your go-to resource for logistical details.

2. **Top Destinations**: For inspiration on where to visit, this section provides detailed descriptions of the must-see cities, regions, and hidden gems in both Spain and Portugal. You'll find key highlights, recommended activities, and lesser-known treasures that you won't want to miss.

3. **Practical Travel Information**: Once you've decided where to go, this section offers all the practical details you need to know—how to get around, where to stay, and the best places to eat. It covers transportation options, accommodation, and local cuisine in both Spain and Portugal.

4. **Suggested Itineraries**: Whether you're short on time or want a fully curated travel route, this section offers customizable itineraries for different types of travelers. From a two-week Iberian tour to a focused exploration of specific regions, these itineraries provide a balance of

must-see sights and off-the-beaten-path experiences.

5. **Cultural Insights**: To truly appreciate Spain and Portugal, understanding their cultures is key. This section delves into local customs, festivals, and traditions, helping you immerse yourself in the way of life. You'll also find helpful language tips, so you can navigate the countries with ease.

6. **Outdoor Adventures**: For nature lovers and adventure seekers, this part of the guide highlights the best outdoor experiences, from hiking the Pyrenees and surfing in the Algarve to discovering the islands of Madeira and the Azores.

7. **Culinary Experiences**: If food is a big part of your travel experience, this section will be your favorite. It explores the gastronomic wonders of Spain and Portugal, offering insights into the best dishes, local markets, and food tours.

8. **Sustainability and Responsible Travel**: Conscious travelers will appreciate this section, which focuses on eco-friendly travel tips, supporting local businesses, and minimizing your environmental impact while exploring Spain and Portugal.

9. **Maps and Visual Guides**: These will help you get oriented and plan your routes, whether you're navigating major cities or embarking on a rural road trip.

10. **Author's Recommendations**: Throughout the guide, you'll find personal recommendations for places to visit, eat, and stay, based on firsthand experiences and insider knowledge.

Use this guide as both a resource and inspiration for your travels. Each section is designed to provide the practical details you need while also offering a deeper appreciation of the rich histories, diverse landscapes, and vibrant cultures of Spain and Portugal. Whether you're a first-time visitor or a seasoned traveler returning for more, this guide will help you plan a memorable and fulfilling trip.

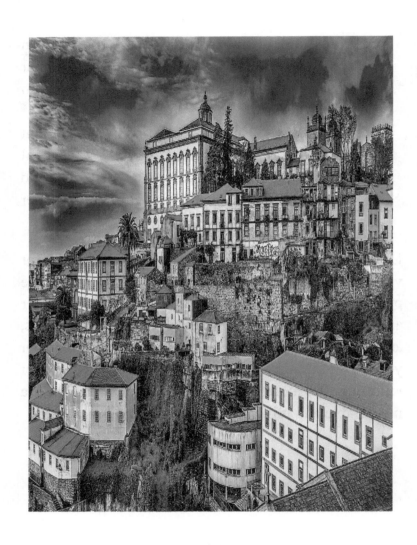

CHAPTER 1

Planning Your Trip

Best Time to Visit Spain and Portugal

The best time to visit Spain and Portugal largely depends on your preferences for weather, crowds, and the activities you wish to pursue. Both countries have diverse climates due to their varied landscapes, but understanding the seasonal patterns will help you plan the ideal trip.

Spring (March to May):

Why Visit: Spring is considered one of the best times to visit both Spain and Portugal. Temperatures are mild, ranging between 15°C and 25°C (59°F to 77°F), and the landscapes are lush and vibrant with blooming flowers.

Where to Go: Cities like Seville, Lisbon, and Barcelona come alive with festivals, such as Spain's Semana Santa (Holy Week) and the Feria de Abril in Seville. Spring is also an excellent time for visiting Portugal's Douro Valley and Spain's wine regions before the summer heat sets in.

Ideal For: Sightseeing, outdoor activities like hiking, and cultural festivals without the high tourist crowds.

Summer (June to August):

Why Visit: Summer is peak tourist season, with sunny weather and long days perfect for beach lovers. However, it's also the busiest time, with temperatures soaring, especially in southern Spain and Portugal.

Where to Go: Coastal regions like Spain's Costa Brava, Costa del Sol, and the Balearic Islands, as well as Portugal's Algarve, are at their best. The cities can be hot (often above 30°C or 86°F), but this is a great time to visit cooler coastal towns or escape to the north (e.g., Galicia, Asturias in Spain, or the Azores in Portugal).

Ideal For: Beach vacations, coastal getaways, and outdoor adventures like sailing or surfing.

Autumn (September to November):

Why Visit: Autumn is another fantastic time to visit, as the summer crowds diminish, and the weather remains pleasant, with temperatures averaging between 20°C and 28°C (68°F to 82°F).

Where to Go: Wine lovers will enjoy harvest season in Spain's La Rioja and Portugal's Douro Valley. Cities like Madrid, Lisbon, and Porto have pleasant temperatures and fewer tourists.

Ideal For: Wine tours, city exploration, hiking, and outdoor activities.

Winter (December to February):

Why Visit: Winters are generally mild, especially in coastal areas, though inland Spain can get cold, especially in mountainous regions. This is the perfect time to experience the cultural charm of cities without large crowds, and it's also ski season in the Pyrenees and Sierra Nevada mountains.

Where to Go: Southern Spain (Andalusia) and Portugal's Algarve offer mild temperatures, while cities like Barcelona and Lisbon have cooler but comfortable conditions. Winter is also ideal for visiting Spain's Canary Islands, where temperatures remain warm year-round.

Ideal For: City breaks, cultural exploration, skiing, and winter festivals.

Entry Requirements

Both Spain and Portugal are members of the European Union and part of the Schengen Area, meaning they share common entry requirements for foreign travelers.

Passport Requirements:

Travelers from non-EU countries, including the U.S., Canada, Australia, and the U.K., need a passport valid for at least three months beyond their intended departure from the Schengen Area. Ensure your passport is in good condition, as damaged passports may cause issues at the border.

EU citizens only need a valid national ID card to enter Spain and Portugal.

Visa Requirements:

For Schengen Visa-Exempt Countries: Nationals from the U.S., Canada, Australia, and many other countries can enter Spain and Portugal without a visa for stays of up to 90 days within a 180-day period.

For Non-Schengen Visa-Exempt Countries: Travelers from countries that are not part of the Schengen visa-waiver program will need to apply for a short-stay Schengen visa before traveling. This visa allows for up to 90 days in the Schengen Area.

ETIAS (European Travel Information and Authorization System): Beginning in 2024, travelers from visa-exempt countries will need to apply for ETIAS authorization before entering the Schengen Area, including Spain and Portugal. This is a simple online application.

How to Get There

Spain and Portugal are well-connected to the rest of the world and within Europe, offering several ways to reach the Iberian Peninsula.

1. **Flights:**

Major Airports:

Spain: Madrid-Barajas (MAD) and Barcelona-El Prat (BCN) are the two largest international hubs. Other significant airports include Málaga (AGP), Seville (SVQ), and Valencia (VLC).

Portugal: Lisbon Humberto Delgado Airport (LIS) is the largest airport, followed by Porto (OPO) and Faro (FAO), serving the Algarve region.

Direct Flights: Spain and Portugal are well-served by direct international flights from North America, Latin America, Europe, and the Middle East. Many budget airlines also operate within Europe, making Spain and Portugal accessible for short trips from other European countries.

2. Trains:

Spain and Portugal are connected by rail, although high-speed routes are limited between the two. From other European countries, you can reach Spain via France on the high-speed TGV trains (Paris to Barcelona or Madrid).

Portugal's domestic train network is extensive, and the Alfa Pendular high-speed train connects major cities like Lisbon, Porto, and Faro.

3. Ferries:

While less common, ferry routes are available between Spain and North Africa (Morocco), the Balearic Islands, and the Canary Islands. There are also ferries between Spain and the U.K., departing from Bilbao and Santander.

Transportation Options

Planes:

Domestic flights are available for travelers who want to cover large distances quickly, such as traveling from Madrid to the Canary Islands or Lisbon to Porto. Budget airlines like Vueling and Ryanair offer frequent routes within Spain and Portugal.

Trains:

Spain: Spain has an extensive and efficient rail network, especially the high-speed AVE trains that connect major cities like Madrid, Barcelona, Seville, and Valencia. The train system is comfortable, reliable, and a scenic way to travel.

Portugal: Portugal's trains are slower but still an excellent option for connecting cities like Lisbon, Porto, and Faro. The Alfa Pendular is the fastest train service in the country.

Buses:

Spain: The bus network in Spain is comprehensive, often reaching smaller towns and rural areas that trains don't serve. Companies like ALSA and Avanza provide comfortable, long-distance travel.

Portugal: Rede Expressos is Portugal's main bus operator, offering connections between Lisbon, Porto, the Algarve, and smaller towns.

Cars:

Renting a car is an excellent option if you want the freedom to explore rural areas, coastal routes, or off-the-beaten-path destinations. Both Spain and Portugal have well-maintained roads, but parking in city centers can be difficult and expensive.

In Spain, toll roads (autopistas) are common, and the same applies to Portugal. Be aware of toll systems, as some roads require electronic toll payments.

Money and Budgeting

Currency:

Both Spain and Portugal use the Euro (€). Credit cards are widely accepted, but it's useful to carry some cash for smaller purchases, especially in rural areas or for public transport.

Costs:

Accommodation:

Budget travelers can find hostel dorms for around €15-€30 per night. Mid-range hotels average €60-€150, while luxury hotels can cost €200 and up per night.

Meals:

Budget meals (cafés or street food) range from €10-€15. A meal at a mid-range restaurant will cost around €20-€40 per person, while fine dining experiences can exceed €100 per person.

Transport:

Public transport fares are affordable, with single metro or bus tickets costing between €1.50 and €2.50 in major cities. High-speed train tickets between cities (e.g., Madrid to Barcelona) can range from €40-€150, depending on how early you book.

Saving Tips:

Use Public Transport: Spain and Portugal's public transport systems are excellent and much cheaper than renting a car for city-to-city travel.

Free Attractions: Many museums and attractions in Spain and Portugal offer free entry on certain days or times, such as the Prado Museum in Madrid (free entry after 6 p.m.).

Local Markets: To save on meals, consider eating at local markets where you can get fresh produce and affordable street food.

What to Pack

Spring/Summer:

Essentials: Lightweight clothing, comfortable walking shoes, a sunhat, sunglasses, and sunscreen. Pack swimwear if you plan to hit the beaches. Bring a light jacket for cooler evenings.

Footwear: Comfortable shoes are a must for walking around cities or hiking.

Autumn:

Essentials: Layered clothing, a rain jacket, and comfortable walking shoes. Temperatures can vary, so pack both light and warm layers.

Footwear: Waterproof shoes or boots are advisable if you plan to visit rural or mountainous areas.

Winter:

Essentials: A warm coat, scarves, gloves, and layers. While coastal areas remain mild, central Spain and northern Portugal can get cold, especially at night.

Footwear: Sturdy, warm shoes or boots for colder, possibly wet conditions.

General Packing Tips: Always pack travel adapters (Spain and Portugal use the standard European plug type), a reusable water bottle, and copies of important documents (passport, visa). For those visiting rural areas or planning outdoor activities, consider a small backpack for day trips.

CHAPTER 2

Top Destinations in Spain

Madrid

Madrid, the vibrant capital of Spain, is a bustling metropolis known for its rich history, royal heritage, world-class art, and lively urban energy. It's a city where centuries-old traditions coexist with cutting-edge modernity. With grand boulevards, royal palaces, verdant parks, and world-renowned museums, Madrid offers visitors a unique blend of history, culture, and contemporary life.

As the political and cultural heart of Spain, Madrid is a city that attracts all kinds of travelers—from art aficionados and history buffs to food lovers and night owls. With its cosmopolitan atmosphere, the city is also home to an international community, which has influenced everything from its cuisine to its fashion and music scenes.

Highlights: Prado Museum, Royal Palace, Retiro Park

Prado Museum (Museo del Prado)
The Prado Museum is one of the most famous art museums in the world and a must-visit for anyone traveling to Madrid. It houses an extensive collection of European art dating from the 12th to the early 20th centuries, with works by renowned masters such as Francisco Goya, Diego Velázquez, and El Greco. Among its most celebrated pieces are Velázquez's *Las Meninas* and Goya's *The Third of May 1808*.
The museum's collection spans various art movements and includes masterpieces from the Spanish Golden Age, Flemish and Dutch works, and Italian Renaissance paintings. The Prado is not only a

showcase of artistic brilliance but also a journey through the history of European art.

Tip: For a deeper experience, consider joining a guided tour to fully appreciate the context and significance of the works. The museum also offers free entry during the last two hours of operation.

Royal Palace of Madrid (Palacio Real de Madrid)

As one of the largest royal palaces in Europe, the Royal Palace of Madrid is a stunning testament to Spain's regal history. Though it is no longer the official residence of the Spanish royal family (they now live at the smaller Palacio de la Zarzuela), the Royal Palace is still used for official state ceremonies and remains a symbol of Spanish royalty.

The palace boasts over 3,000 rooms, lavishly decorated with tapestries, paintings, and antiques. Visitors can tour several opulent rooms, including the Throne Room, the Royal Armory, and the Royal Pharmacy. Don't miss the grand courtyard, which offers spectacular views of the surrounding cityscape.

Tip: The palace is free to visit on certain days for EU citizens, and the changing of the guard ceremony, which takes place every Wednesday and Saturday, is a sight to behold.

Retiro Park (Parque del Retiro)

Retiro Park is Madrid's green oasis and a perfect spot for relaxation amid sightseeing. Originally a royal garden, Retiro is now one of the largest parks in the city, offering beautiful gardens, peaceful lakes, and tree-lined walkways. The park is home to several notable landmarks, including the Crystal Palace (Palacio de Cristal), a stunning glass pavilion that often hosts art exhibitions.

Visitors can rent rowboats and paddle across the park's large central lake, explore the beautiful Rose Garden (La Rosaleda), or simply relax with a picnic on the expansive lawns. Retiro is also a great place to people-watch, as it's a popular spot for both locals and tourists alike.

Tip: Visit Retiro Park on a Sunday when the park comes alive with street performers, musicians, and local vendors.

Hidden Gems

While Madrid's major attractions are undoubtedly awe-inspiring, some of its charm lies in its hidden corners and off-the-beaten-path locales. Exploring Madrid's vibrant neighborhoods and authentic street markets will give you a true sense of local life and culture.

Local Neighborhoods (Barrios)

La Latina: This lively neighborhood is the epicenter of Madrid's tapas culture and nightlife. La Latina's narrow, winding streets are filled with tapas bars, cafés, and bodegas, making it the perfect place for a casual evening of food and drinks. Plaza de la Cebada and Plaza de la Paja are great spots to sit outside and enjoy the lively atmosphere. On Sundays, La Latina is the site of the famous El Rastro flea market.

Malasaña: Known as the hipster neighborhood of Madrid, Malasaña is filled with trendy boutiques, street art, and vintage shops. It's a cultural hotspot with a bohemian vibe, offering unique coffee shops, galleries, and independent stores. Malasaña was once the center of Madrid's La Movida Madrileña countercultural movement in the 1980s, and today it retains its youthful, creative energy.

Lavapiés: This multicultural neighborhood is a melting pot of different cultures, with influences from Africa, Asia, and Latin America. Lavapiés is known for its alternative art scene, vibrant festivals, and international food. Wander through the streets to discover colorful murals, quirky cafés, and affordable restaurants offering cuisine from around the world.

Chueca: Chueca is Madrid's LGBTQ+ district, celebrated for its inclusive, lively, and artistic atmosphere. It's home to chic bars, eclectic restaurants, and upscale boutiques. Chueca is also a center for Madrid's LGBTQ+ Pride celebrations, one of the largest in Europe.

Tip: Madrid is a city that rewards wandering—stroll through these neighborhoods without a strict agenda, stopping at local cafés, browsing boutiques, and enjoying spontaneous encounters with street performers or impromptu art exhibits.

- **Street Markets**

El Rastro: Held every Sunday in the La Latina neighborhood, El Rastro is Madrid's most famous flea market and one of the largest in Europe. Stalls selling everything from vintage clothing and antiques to handmade crafts and artwork line the streets. The market stretches from Plaza de Cascorro to Ronda de Toledo, with plenty of bars and cafés nearby to stop for a drink after browsing.

Mercado de San Miguel: For food lovers, the Mercado de San Miguel is a must-visit. Located near Plaza Mayor, this historic market is a paradise for anyone interested in sampling traditional Spanish food.

The market offers a wide range of tapas, from fresh seafood and jamón ibérico to cheeses, olives, and churros with chocolate. It's an excellent spot to experience Spain's culinary traditions in a vibrant, social atmosphere.

Mercado de San Fernando: Located in the Lavapiés neighborhood, this lesser-known market is a hidden gem, offering a more local experience than the often tourist-filled Mercado de San Miguel. Here you'll find organic produce, gourmet food stalls, and independent shops selling books, clothing, and home goods. The market also features pop-up food stalls where you can enjoy dishes from around the world.

Tip: To get the best experience from the markets, arrive early to avoid the crowds and spend time talking to the vendors. Many will be happy to share stories about their products, whether it's hand-crafted jewelry or locally sourced cheeses.

Madrid is a city of contrasts—where royal splendor meets contemporary culture, and world-famous museums sit alongside vibrant street markets. Whether you're visiting for its historic landmarks or to discover its hidden neighborhoods, Madrid offers an immersive cultural experience that will captivate and inspire.

Barcelona

Barcelona, the cosmopolitan capital of Spain's Catalonia region, is a city of boundless energy, artistic flair, and architectural grandeur. Renowned for its stunning Modernist buildings, sun-kissed beaches, and rich cultural heritage, Barcelona offers an irresistible combination of history, art, and laid-back Mediterranean vibes. Whether you're a lover of architecture, a beachgoer, or a history buff, Barcelona has something for everyone.

The city is famously associated with the architectural genius Antoni Gaudí, whose masterpieces, including the still-unfinished **La Sagrada Familia**, have become iconic symbols of Barcelona. Beyond its architectural wonders, Barcelona is home to bustling markets, picturesque plazas, and a vibrant food scene that combines traditional Catalan dishes with innovative culinary delights.

Highlights: La Sagrada Familia, Park Güell, Gothic Quarter

La Sagrada Familia

Perhaps the most iconic sight in Barcelona, **La Sagrada Familia** is an architectural marvel and a symbol of Gaudí's visionary genius. Construction on the basilica began in 1882, and despite still being incomplete, it's one of the most visited monuments in Spain. Gaudí's unique interpretation of Gothic and Art Nouveau architecture is on full display in the church's intricate façades, soaring towers, and awe-inspiring interior.

Inside, visitors are greeted by a spectacular play of light and color as sunlight filters through the vividly colored stained glass windows, casting a kaleidoscope of hues across the basilica's columns and vaulted ceilings. The basilica's Nativity Façade is dedicated to the birth of Christ and represents Gaudí's deep religious faith, while the Passion Façade is a more austere representation of Christ's suffering.

Tip: To avoid long lines, book your tickets in advance online, and consider a guided tour to fully appreciate the symbolism and history behind Gaudí's design. For panoramic views of Barcelona, take the elevator up one of the basilica's towers.

Park Güell

Another masterpiece by Antoni Gaudí, **Park Güell** is a whimsical, colorful park that overlooks the city and offers sweeping views of Barcelona and the Mediterranean Sea. Originally conceived as a housing development, the park became a public space in the early 20th century, showcasing Gaudí's imaginative use of organic shapes, vibrant mosaics, and architectural innovation.

The park's main terrace, known for its undulating bench covered in broken ceramic tiles (trencadís), is a prime spot for relaxing and taking in the breathtaking view. Other highlights of the park include the famous mosaic lizard sculpture, known as "El Drac," and the Hypostyle Hall, a forest of stone columns that support the park's upper level.

Park Güell is a UNESCO World Heritage site and one of the finest examples of Gaudí's work, blending nature with architectural brilliance.

Tip: Since Park Güell has both free and paid areas, it's worth booking tickets in advance to visit the monumental zone where Gaudí's most famous works are located. Early mornings and late afternoons are the best times to visit to avoid crowds and enjoy the serene atmosphere.

Gothic Quarter (Barri Gòtic)

The **Gothic Quarter** is the historic heart of Barcelona, where narrow medieval streets, ancient Roman ruins, and towering Gothic buildings take visitors on a journey through the city's rich history. Strolling through the labyrinthine streets, you'll discover hidden squares, such as **Plaça Reial**, and centuries-old buildings, including **Barcelona Cathedral** (Catedral de la Santa Creu i Santa Eulàlia), with its striking Gothic architecture.

The neighborhood is filled with history at every turn, from the remains of Roman walls to the **Plaça del Rei**, where Christopher Columbus is said to have reported back to the Catholic Monarchs after his first voyage to the Americas. The area is also home to the **Jewish Quarter (El Call)**, one of the oldest parts of the city, where you can visit the **Ancient Synagogue of Barcelona**.

Beyond its historical significance, the Gothic Quarter is alive with modern-day culture. It's a hub for shopping, dining, and street performers, and it's known for its vibrant atmosphere day and night. From quirky boutiques to cozy tapas bars, the Gothic Quarter seamlessly blends the old with the new.

Tip: Be sure to explore the tiny alleyways and courtyards that are easy to miss but offer a glimpse into Barcelona's medieval past. Guided walking tours are a great way to learn about the rich history and legends of the area.

Day Trips

While Barcelona

itself is full of attractions, its surrounding areas offer stunning landscapes and cultural experiences that make for perfect day trips. Two of the most popular excursions are to **Montserrat** and the **Costa Brava**.

Montserrat

Nestled in the mountains about an hour outside of Barcelona, **Montserrat** is a sacred site and one of the most striking natural landscapes in Catalonia. The mountain is home to the **Benedictine Abbey of Santa Maria de Montserrat**, where the famous statue of the **Black Madonna (La Moreneta)**, Catalonia's patron saint, is venerated. Pilgrims and tourists alike visit the monastery to see the Black Madonna and hear the **Escolania Boys' Choir**, one of the oldest in Europe.

In addition to its religious significance, Montserrat offers numerous hiking trails that lead to panoramic viewpoints, including the summit of **Sant Jeroni**, which provides breathtaking views of the surrounding countryside and the Pyrenees on clear days. The jagged peaks of Montserrat create a dramatic backdrop, making it a must-visit for nature lovers and those seeking spiritual peace.

Tip: To reach Montserrat, you can take a train from Barcelona and then a cable car or funicular up the mountain. Plan your visit in the morning to enjoy the quieter atmosphere before the main crowds arrive.

Costa Brava

Just a short drive from Barcelona, the **Costa Brava** is one of Spain's most stunning coastal regions, known for its rugged cliffs, crystal-clear waters, and charming seaside towns. Stretching from **Blanes** to the French border, the Costa Brava offers a perfect combination of beautiful beaches, scenic hiking trails, and quaint fishing villages.

One of the highlights of the Costa Brava is the town of **Cadaqués**, a picturesque village famous for its white-washed houses, cobbled streets, and its connection to the surrealist artist **Salvador Dalí**, who spent much of his life there. You can visit the **Dalí House-Museum** in nearby **Portlligat**, where the artist lived and worked.

The region also boasts hidden coves, such as **Cala Sa Tuna** and **Cala Pola**, ideal for swimming, snorkeling, or simply relaxing by the Mediterranean Sea. Hiking the **Cami de Ronda**, a coastal path that winds along the cliffs, is a popular way to explore the natural beauty of the area.

Tip: While some beaches can get crowded in the summer months, visiting during the shoulder seasons (spring or early fall) will allow you to enjoy the beauty of the Costa Brava with fewer crowds. You can reach the Costa Brava by car or bus from Barcelona.

Barcelona's unique blend of artistic heritage, stunning architecture, and sun-soaked beaches make it a top destination in Spain. Whether you're admiring Gaudí's surreal creations, wandering the historic streets of the Gothic Quarter, or enjoying the laid-back charm of its beaches, Barcelona is a city that promises endless discoveries. With easy access to breathtaking day trips like Montserrat and Costa Brava, the city offers both cultural and natural adventures, ensuring that every traveler's experience is unforgettable.

Seville

Seville, the capital of Spain's Andalusia region, is a city steeped in history, culture, and romance. Known for its passionate flamenco performances, Moorish architecture, and festive spirit, Seville offers an authentic taste of southern Spain. Its winding streets, vibrant plazas, and iconic landmarks make it one of the most enchanting cities in the country.

A city where cultures have mingled for centuries, Seville is a living testament to Spain's rich history, with influences from the Romans, Moors, and Christians all evident in its architecture and traditions. From the grandeur of the **Alcázar** to the vibrant energy of flamenco shows, Seville is a place where history comes alive and tradition coexists with modern life.

Seville is also known for its relaxed lifestyle, offering travelers a chance to slow down and savor the beauty of its surroundings—whether it's a leisurely afternoon in one of its many lush gardens or enjoying tapas at a local bar. The warmth of the Sevillanos, combined with the city's cultural treasures, makes Seville a must-visit destination for anyone exploring Spain.

Highlights: Alcázar, Seville Cathedral, Plaza de España

Alcázar of Seville (Real Alcázar de Sevilla)

The **Alcázar of Seville** is a breathtaking palace complex that embodies the fusion of Moorish and Christian architectural styles, a testament to the city's long and varied history. Originally built as a Moorish fortress in the 10th century, the Alcázar has been expanded and transformed over the centuries, serving as a royal residence for various Spanish monarchs.

Today, it remains one of the oldest palaces in Europe still in use, with parts of it functioning as a residence for the Spanish royal family when they visit Seville.

The palace is a masterpiece of **Mudéjar architecture**, with intricately carved arches, stunning courtyards, and beautiful gardens. One of the most famous areas is the **Patio de las Doncellas (Courtyard of the Maidens)**, known for its tranquil reflecting pool and ornate arches. The **Salón de Embajadores (Hall of Ambassadors)**, with its dazzling golden dome, showcases the wealth and power of the kings who once held court here.

The **Alcázar Gardens** are equally impressive, featuring a mix of lush greenery, fountains, and carefully manicured paths that invite visitors to take a peaceful stroll. The gardens also offer views of the palace's architecture from different angles, providing a perfect backdrop for photographs.

Tip: The Alcázar can get quite busy, so it's best to book your tickets online and visit early in the morning or late in the afternoon to avoid the crowds. Game of Thrones fans may also recognize parts of the Alcázar, as it was used as a filming location for the fictional Kingdom of Dorne.

Seville Cathedral (Catedral de Sevilla)

Seville Cathedral is the largest Gothic cathedral in the world and an architectural marvel that dominates the city's skyline. Built on the site of a former mosque, the cathedral is a UNESCO World Heritage site and a symbol of Seville's rich religious history. Its most famous feature is the towering **Giralda** bell tower, originally constructed as a minaret during the city's Moorish period.

The cathedral's interior is just as grand as its exterior, with soaring vaulted ceilings, intricate stained glass windows, and a treasure trove of religious art and artifacts. One of the cathedral's most significant relics is the **tomb of Christopher Columbus**, whose remains are interred in a grand monument held aloft by four figures representing the kingdoms of Spain.

Visitors can also climb the **Giralda Tower**, which offers spectacular panoramic views of the city. The ascent is relatively easy, as the tower was designed with ramps rather than stairs, allowing the muezzin to ride a horse to the top during the Moorish period.

Tip: Don't miss the **Patio de los Naranjos (Courtyard of the Orange Trees)**, a peaceful space that reflects the mosque's Islamic origins. The cathedral also offers night tours, allowing visitors to experience its grandeur in a more intimate and less crowded setting.

Plaza de España

Plaza de España is one of Seville's most iconic landmarks and a stunning example of **Renaissance Revival** and **Regionalist architecture**. Built in 1928 for the Ibero-American Exposition of 1929, the plaza is an impressive semi-circular structure surrounded by a canal crossed by ornate bridges, often referred to as "the Venice of Seville." The central building is adorned with ceramic tiles, wrought ironwork, and grand colonnades, making it one of the most photogenic spots in the city.

The plaza is not just a visual marvel; it's also a celebration of Spain's provinces, with tiled alcoves along the perimeter of the building representing each of the country's regions. Visitors can explore these alcoves, each uniquely decorated with scenes from the region's history and culture. The **canal** that runs through the plaza offers visitors the chance to rent small boats and row around, adding a playful element to the experience.

Plaza de España is surrounded by the lush **Parque de María Luisa**, which is perfect for a leisurely stroll, a picnic, or simply relaxing in the shade of its towering trees. The park features beautiful gardens, fountains, and hidden corners, making it a serene escape from the bustling city.

Tip: Visit the plaza during sunset when the warm light enhances the beauty of the tiles and creates a magical atmosphere. The plaza is also a popular location for live performances, so you may come across impromptu flamenco shows or musicians.

Flamenco

Flamenco is more than just a dance or music genre—it's the heartbeat of Seville and an integral part of the city's cultural identity. With roots in Andalusia's gypsy, Moorish, and Jewish cultures, flamenco is an art form that expresses deep emotion through song (**cante**), dance (**baile**), and guitar playing (**toque**).

Seville is one of the best places in Spain to experience authentic flamenco. Visitors can enjoy performances in intimate settings at **tablaos** (flamenco venues), where passionate dancers and musicians pour their heart and soul into every movement and note. The **Barrio de Triana** neighborhood, located across the **Guadalquivir River**, is known as the birthplace of flamenco and is home to many tablaos, as well as traditional workshops where artisans create flamenco guitars and tiles.

For those who want to dive deeper into the world of flamenco, the **Museo del Baile Flamenco** offers an excellent overview of the history and evolution of the art form. The museum also hosts live performances that showcase the different styles of flamenco.

Tip: For an authentic flamenco experience, avoid touristy spots and instead seek out smaller, local venues in Triana or the city center. These intimate performances allow for a more personal connection with the art form.

Seville's Timeless Charm

What truly sets Seville apart is its ability to transport visitors to a different time, where Moorish palaces, grand cathedrals, and vibrant plazas coexist with the rhythms of daily life. The city's charming streets, filled with orange trees and colorful facades, invite you to wander at a leisurely pace, discovering hidden gems along the way.

Seville's calendar is filled with lively festivals, such as **Semana Santa (Holy Week)** and the **Feria de Abril (April Fair)**, both of which showcase the city's deep-rooted traditions and festive spirit. During these times, the streets come alive with processions, music, and dancing, offering travelers a unique opportunity to experience Seville's culture firsthand.

Whether you're mesmerized by a flamenco performance, exploring the halls of the Alcázar, or simply enjoying tapas in a local plaza, Seville's history, charm, and soul-stirring energy will leave a lasting impression on anyone who visits. It's a city that invites you to slow down, savor the moment, and immerse yourself in its timeless beauty.

Granada

Granada, nestled at the foot of the Sierra Nevada

mountains in southern Spain, is one of the most captivating cities in Andalusia. It is a place where Spain's rich Islamic past is still vividly preserved, and its fascinating blend of cultures, landscapes, and history make it a unique destination. Known as the last stronghold of the Moors in Spain, Granada offers visitors a deep dive into the region's Moorish heritage, embodied most dramatically by the Alhambra, one of the most remarkable monuments in the world.

Granada is also a city of contrasts. Beyond its magnificent palaces and Islamic architecture, it boasts a vibrant, modern Spanish culture, with lively tapas bars, flamenco performances, and a student-friendly atmosphere thanks to its historic university. Granada's position as a crossroads between different civilizations has left it with a layered identity, reflected in its art, cuisine, and architecture.

Highlights: The Alhambra, Generalife Gardens, Sacromonte

The Alhambra
The Alhambra, a UNESCO World Heritage site, is Granada's crown jewel and one of Spain's most visited landmarks. This sprawling palace and fortress complex was built in the 13th and 14th centuries by the Nasrid Dynasty, the last Muslim rulers of Spain, and it

remains an outstanding example of Islamic architecture in Europe.

The Alhambra is a masterpiece of craftsmanship, combining delicate stucco work, intricately carved wood, and breathtaking tile mosaics. As you wander through the palace, you'll discover a series of rooms and courtyards designed to inspire awe. One of the most famous areas is the **Palacio de los Leones (Palace of the Lions)**, where a stunning central fountain, supported by 12 marble lions, stands as a symbol of strength and power. The courtyard surrounding the fountain is an exquisite example of Nasrid architecture, with its slender columns, graceful arches, and carved details.

Another must-see area of the Alhambra is the **Hall of the Ambassadors (Salón de los Embajadores)**, located in the **Palacio de Comares**. This grand reception room was where the sultans received dignitaries and conducted state affairs. Its striking ceiling, made of cedarwood in the shape of a star, and the intricate geometric patterns on the walls, exemplify the beauty and complexity of Moorish design.

Beyond the architecture, the Alhambra's significance lies in its representation of the complex history of medieval Spain, where Islamic, Jewish, and Christian cultures coexisted and influenced one another. The fortress was eventually taken by the Catholic

Monarchs, Ferdinand and Isabella, in 1492, marking the end of Muslim rule in Spain.

Tip: The Alhambra is one of Spain's most popular attractions, so booking tickets well in advance is essential, especially during peak tourist seasons. Consider visiting early in the morning or in the evening for a more tranquil experience, and don't miss the breathtaking views of the city and the Sierra Nevada mountains from the fortress.

Generalife Gardens
Adjacent to the Alhambra, the **Generalife Gardens** offer a peaceful escape from the grandeur of the palaces. Built as a summer retreat for the Nasrid rulers, the Generalife is a serene paradise of meticulously landscaped gardens, fountains, and reflecting pools. Its name is thought to mean "the architect's garden," and it is easy to see why this space was designed as a place of reflection and relaxation.

The **Patio de la Acequia** is the heart of the Generalife, where a long pool framed by myrtle hedges and splashing fountains creates a soothing ambiance. Surrounding the pool are arcades and pavilions that provide shade and shelter, while the gentle sound of running water contributes to the garden's tranquil atmosphere. The **Patio de los Cipreses (Court of the**

Cypresses), with its ancient cypress trees and lily-strewn pond, is another picturesque spot.

As you stroll through the gardens, you'll be treated to stunning views of the Alhambra's red walls and the city of Granada below. The contrast between the lush greenery of the Generalife and the arid mountains in the distance highlights the ingenuity of Islamic garden design, which sought to create oases of beauty and calm in the heart of a dry, hot landscape.

Tip: Allow plenty of time to explore the Generalife Gardens, as their beauty lies not only in the larger features but in the small details—the play of light on the water, the scent of flowers, and the sound of birds. If possible, visit in the early morning or late afternoon to avoid the midday heat.

Sacromonte

Just beyond the bustling city center of Granada lies the neighborhood of **Sacromonte**, a unique and historic area known for its **cave dwellings** and vibrant **flamenco culture**. This hillside barrio is where many of Granada's **Roma (gypsy)** population settled after the Reconquista, and it has since become synonymous with traditional flamenco music and dance.

Sacromonte is a strikingly picturesque area, with its whitewashed cave homes built directly into the hillsides. These **caves**, known as **cuevas**, have been inhabited for centuries and are still home to many locals today. Some of these cave houses have been converted into museums, offering visitors a glimpse into how people lived in these unique structures, which are surprisingly cool in the summer and warm in the winter.

Flamenco is deeply rooted in the culture of Sacromonte, and visitors can attend authentic performances at **tablaos** (flamenco venues) located in the caves. These intimate settings provide the perfect backdrop for experiencing the raw passion and intensity of flamenco, as the haunting sounds of the **cante jondo** (deep song) and the rhythmic **zapateado** (footwork) echo through the stone walls.

Sacromonte is also a great place to enjoy sweeping views of the Alhambra and the Albayzín, another historic district in Granada. As the sun sets and the city lights up, the view from Sacromonte's hilltop vantage points is one of the most iconic in all of Spain.

Tip: For the best flamenco experience, seek out smaller, local venues in Sacromonte where the performances feel more personal and less commercialized. You can also combine a visit to Sacromonte with a walk through the **Albayzín**, Granada's old Moorish quarter, known for its narrow cobblestone streets and stunning views of the Alhambra.

Granada's Moorish Legacy

Granada's charm and allure lie in its ability to transport visitors back to a time when it was the flourishing heart of Al-Andalus, the Muslim-ruled territory in medieval Spain. The city's architectural and cultural landscape is a blend of Islamic, Christian, and Jewish influences, a reflection of its complex past.

One of the most evocative areas to explore is the **Albayzín**, a UNESCO-listed neighborhood that was once the heart of the city's Moorish population. As you wander through its winding streets, you'll discover hidden patios, old mosques converted into churches, and scenic lookout points like the **Mirador de San Nicolás**, which offers stunning views of the Alhambra against the backdrop of the Sierra Nevada.

Granada is also famous for its **tapas** culture, where many bars offer free tapas with drinks. This tradition makes dining out in Granada a social and culinary adventure, where visitors can savor local specialties while hopping from bar to bar.

Granada's rich history, stunning architecture, and vibrant cultural scene make it one of Spain's most captivating cities. From the awe-inspiring beauty of the Alhambra and Generalife Gardens to the soulful flamenco of Sacromonte, Granada offers travelers an unforgettable journey through Spain's Moorish past. Whether exploring ancient palaces or wandering the labyrinthine streets of the Albayzín, visitors are sure to be enchanted by the city's unique blend of old-world charm and modern vibrancy.

Valencia

Valencia, the third-largest city in Spain, is a vibrant blend of the traditional and the modern, where the rich cultural heritage of the past coexists with cutting-edge architecture and innovative projects. Nestled on the eastern coast of Spain along the Mediterranean Sea, Valencia is known for its stunning beaches, bustling markets, and a culinary scene that has given birth to the world-famous dish, **paella**.

The city boasts an array of historical sites, a thriving arts scene, and an inviting atmosphere that reflects its Mediterranean roots. Valencia is often considered a hidden gem in Spain, offering travelers a unique experience that captures the essence of Spanish culture while remaining less crowded than other popular destinations like Barcelona and Madrid.

Highlights: City of Arts and Sciences, Valencia Cathedral, Beaches

City of Arts and Sciences (Ciudad de las Artes y las Ciencias)

The **City of Arts and Sciences** is Valencia's most iconic modern landmark, showcasing an extraordinary blend of futuristic architecture and cultural attractions. Designed by architect Santiago Calatrava and Félix Candela, this stunning complex spans over 350,000 square meters and features several futuristic structures, each dedicated to different aspects of science and the arts.

L'Oceanogràfic: This is the largest aquarium in Europe and one of the highlights of the City of Arts and Sciences. It is home to thousands of marine species, including dolphins, sharks, and sea turtles, housed in meticulously designed habitats that replicate their natural environments. Visitors can explore underwater tunnels, enjoy live shows, and even dine underwater at the restaurant.

Museo de las Ciencias Príncipe Felipe: This interactive science museum is designed to make science accessible and fun for visitors of all ages. The exhibits cover a wide range of topics, from biology to physics, and encourage hands-on learning through interactive displays and demonstrations. Don't miss the IMAX theater, which screens educational films in stunning 3D.

Palau de les Arts Reina Sofía: This grand opera house and cultural center is a stunning example of modern architecture and hosts a variety of performances, including opera, ballet, and concerts. The acoustics and design have made it one of the premier venues for the performing arts in Spain.

Tip: To fully appreciate the City of Arts and Sciences, consider purchasing a combined ticket that grants access to multiple attractions. The complex is particularly magical at night when the buildings are illuminated, making for a picturesque setting for evening strolls.

Valencia Cathedral (Catedral de Valencia)

The **Valencia Cathedral**, located in the heart of the city, is a stunning architectural marvel that reflects various styles, including Romanesque, Gothic, and Baroque. Dating back to the 13th century, the cathedral is built on the site of a former mosque and serves as a reminder of Valencia's rich history of religious and cultural fusion.

The cathedral is famous for housing the **Holy Grail**, believed by some to be the actual chalice used by Jesus at the Last Supper. Visitors can explore the cathedral's interior, which features impressive chapels, intricate altarpieces, and stunning stained glass windows that bathe the space in colorful light.

The **Miguelete Tower**, a symbol of Valencia, stands adjacent to the cathedral. Climbing its 207 steps rewards visitors with panoramic views of the city, the Turia Gardens, and the Mediterranean Sea in the distance.

Tip: Visit the cathedral early in the morning to enjoy a more peaceful atmosphere and to attend the daily mass, which is a moving experience. The cathedral is also beautifully lit in the evening, making it a perfect subject for photography.

Beaches

Valencia boasts several beautiful beaches along its coastline, making it an ideal destination for sun-seekers and water sports enthusiasts. The city's beaches are easily accessible from the city center, allowing visitors to enjoy a day of relaxation by the Mediterranean Sea.

Playa de la Malvarrosa: This is Valencia's most famous beach, known for its wide sandy shore and lively promenade lined with beach bars (**chiringuitos**) and restaurants. Visitors can rent sun loungers, enjoy beach volleyball, or simply relax under the sun with a refreshing drink. The promenade is perfect for a leisurely stroll, especially at sunset when the sky is painted with vibrant colors.

Playa de las Arenas: Located next to Malvarrosa, Playa de las Arenas is another popular beach that offers a vibrant atmosphere. Here, visitors can find numerous seafood restaurants where they can indulge in delicious paella while enjoying views of the ocean.

Tip: If you prefer a quieter beach experience, consider heading to **Playa de la Patacona**, just north of

Malvarrosa. This beach is less crowded and offers a more relaxed vibe, making it an ideal spot for families or those looking to escape the busier tourist areas.

Valencia's Culinary Scene

Valencia is renowned for its cuisine, with **paella** being the star dish. This traditional rice dish originates from Valencia and is typically made with a variety of ingredients, including chicken, rabbit, and seasonal vegetables, all cooked in a distinctive **socarrat** (crispy bottom). While there are many variations of paella, the best place to enjoy an authentic dish is at a local restaurant or beachside chiringuito.

Aside from paella, Valencia offers a diverse culinary scene that celebrates both traditional and modern cuisine. Be sure to try local specialties such as **horchata**, a refreshing drink made from tiger nuts, and **fartons**, sweet pastries that are perfect for dipping in horchata.

Tip: To truly experience Valencia's food culture, join a cooking class where you can learn to make paella yourself, or take a food tour that explores the city's vibrant markets, such as **Mercado Central**, where you can sample fresh produce, meats, and local delicacies.

Valencia

Valencia is famous for its lively festivals, the most notable being **Las Fallas**, a week-long celebration held in March that culminates in the burning of giant papier-mâché sculptures. This spectacular event is characterized by parades, fireworks, and street parties, attracting visitors from around the world. The atmosphere during Las Fallas is electric, with locals and tourists alike participating in the festivities.

Another important celebration is **La Tomatina**, held in the nearby town of Buñol in August. This world-famous tomato-throwing festival is a fun and messy event that attracts thousands of participants who engage in a massive tomato fight.

Tip: If you plan to visit Valencia during a festival, make accommodations well in advance, as hotels fill up quickly, and be prepared for an unforgettable experience filled with music, laughter, and cultural immersion.

Valencia is a city that seamlessly blends its rich historical heritage with modern innovations, offering visitors a unique glimpse into Spanish culture and Mediterranean life. From the striking architecture of the City of Arts and Sciences to the historic charm of the Valencia Cathedral and the relaxing beaches along the coast, Valencia captivates travelers with its diverse offerings and vibrant atmosphere. Whether you're indulging in delicious cuisine, enjoying a day at the beach, or participating in lively festivals, Valencia promises an unforgettable experience that reflects the heart and soul of Spain.

CHAPTER 3

Top Destinations in Portugal

Portugal is blessed with a stunning coastline, picturesque islands, and a diverse landscape that captivates visitors. Among its most sought-after regions are the Algarve, Madeira, and the Azores, each offering unique experiences and breathtaking natural beauty.

Algarve

The Algarve, located in the southernmost region of Portugal, is renowned for its stunning beaches, dramatic cliffs, and charming fishing villages. With a warm Mediterranean climate, the Algarve is a popular destination for sun-seekers and outdoor enthusiasts alike.

Ponta da Piedade: This iconic natural landmark near Lagos features striking limestone cliffs, sea caves, and turquoise waters. Visitors can explore the coastline by boat, kayak, or on foot, taking in the breathtaking views of the cliffs and the Atlantic Ocean. The area is particularly picturesque at sunset, when the rocks are illuminated in golden hues.

Benagil Caves: Accessible only by water, the Benagil Caves are a series of stunning sea caves located along the coastline. The most famous cave, known as the **Benagil Cave**, features a large hole in its roof that lets in sunlight, creating a magical atmosphere inside. Visitors can reach the caves by kayak or by joining a boat tour, allowing them to explore the unique rock formations and hidden beaches.

Sagres: Situated at the southwestern tip of the Algarve, Sagres is known for its dramatic landscapes and historical significance. The **Sagres Fortress**, built in the 15th century, offers panoramic views of the rugged coastline and the Atlantic Ocean. The nearby **Cape St. Vincent** is the westernmost point of mainland Europe and is known for its stunning cliffs and breathtaking sunsets. Sagres is also popular among surfers, with numerous beaches offering excellent waves.

Tip: The Algarve is dotted with charming towns and villages, such as **Lagos**, **Albufeira**, and **Tavira**, each with its own unique character, beautiful architecture, and local cuisine. Be sure to explore the local markets and enjoy fresh seafood dishes, including grilled sardines and cataplana.

Madeira

Madeira, often referred to as the "Pearl of the Atlantic," is an archipelago situated off the northwest coast of Africa. Known for its lush landscapes, rugged mountains, and stunning coastal views, Madeira is a paradise for nature lovers and adventure seekers.

Laurisilva Forest: This UNESCO World Heritage Site is one of the last remaining laurel forests in the world. It is characterized by dense vegetation, diverse flora, and unique wildlife. Visitors can hike through the forest along well-marked levadas (irrigation channels) that offer breathtaking views of the island's natural beauty. The Levada do Caldeirão Verde is particularly popular, leading to a stunning waterfall surrounded by lush greenery.

Cabo Girão: One of the highest sea cliffs in Europe, Cabo Girão rises 580 meters above the Atlantic Ocean and offers spectacular panoramic views. The glass skywalk allows visitors to look down at the cliffs and the ocean below, creating a thrilling experience. The area is surrounded by beautiful terraced fields and is an excellent spot for photography.

Funchal: The capital city of Madeira, Funchal is a vibrant blend of modernity and tradition. The city is known for its beautiful botanical gardens, charming streets, and lively market, the **Mercado dos Lavradores**, where you can find fresh produce, flowers, and local delicacies. Don't miss the opportunity to take a cable car ride to the **Monte Palace Gardens**, which offer stunning views of the city and the coastline.

Tip: Madeira is famous for its wine, so be sure to visit local wineries for tastings and to learn about the winemaking process. The island also hosts various festivals throughout the year, including the **Madeira Flower Festival** and the **New Year's Eve Fireworks**, which are a spectacular sight.

Azores

The Azores, an archipelago located in the mid-Atlantic, is known for its stunning landscapes, geothermal activity, and rich biodiversity. With lush greenery, volcanic craters, and dramatic coastlines, the Azores are a haven for outdoor enthusiasts and nature lovers.

Sete Cidades: This stunning volcanic caldera on São Miguel Island features two crater lakes, one blue and one green, surrounded by lush hills. Visitors can hike or drive to viewpoints such as **Vista do Rei** for breathtaking panoramic views of the lakes and the surrounding landscape. The area offers numerous hiking trails and opportunities for outdoor activities like kayaking and cycling.

Furnas: Famous for its geothermal activity, Furnas is a picturesque village located in a volcanic valley. Visitors can explore the hot springs, fumaroles, and mineral-rich waters, and even witness the traditional cooking method called **cozido**, where meat and vegetables are slow-cooked underground using the geothermal heat. The **Terra Nostra Botanical Park** is also a must-visit, featuring beautiful gardens and a natural hot spring pool.

Pico Island: Home to Portugal's highest peak, Mount Pico, this island is known for its stunning volcanic landscapes and vineyards. The island offers excellent hiking opportunities, with trails leading to the summit of Mount Pico, where hikers are rewarded with breathtaking views of the surrounding islands and ocean. The UNESCO-listed vineyards on Pico are also a highlight, where unique grape-growing methods are employed in the volcanic soil.

Tip: The Azores are ideal for whale watching, with various species of whales and dolphins spotted in the surrounding waters. Several companies offer boat tours for an unforgettable wildlife experience.

Portugal's diverse landscapes, from the sun-kissed beaches of the Algarve to the lush greenery of Madeira and the volcanic beauty of the Azores, provide a wealth of experiences for travelers. Each destination offers its own unique charm, rich history, and breathtaking natural beauty, making Portugal a captivating country to explore. Whether you are relaxing on a beach, hiking through mountains, or indulging in local cuisine, Portugal promises unforgettable adventures for every traveler.

CHAPTER 4

Practical Travel Information

When traveling through Spain and Portugal, having practical travel information can significantly enhance your experience. Both countries are well-equipped with various transportation options, making it easy to explore their stunning landscapes, vibrant cities, and rich cultures. Here's a comprehensive guide to getting around Spain and Portugal.

Getting Around Spain and Portugal

Traveling within Spain and Portugal is convenient, with a range of transportation options to suit different needs and budgets. Here's a detailed overview of the best ways to navigate these beautiful countries.

Spain: The Spanish high-speed rail network, known as **AVE (Alta Velocidad Española)**, is one of the most advanced in the world, offering fast and efficient service between major cities. With speeds reaching up to 300 km/h (186 mph), the AVE connects cities like Madrid, Barcelona, Seville, Valencia, and Málaga, allowing for quick travel.

Booking: Tickets can be purchased online through the Renfe website or at train stations. It's advisable to book in advance, especially for popular routes, as prices can vary significantly depending on how early you buy your tickets.

Regional Lines: In addition to high-speed trains, Spain has an extensive network of regional trains connecting smaller towns and cities. These trains are generally more affordable and provide a comfortable way to explore the countryside.

Portugal: The Portuguese rail system, operated by **Comboios de Portugal (CP)**, offers a mix of urban and intercity trains. The Alfa Pendular service connects major cities like Lisbon, Porto, and Faro, providing a comfortable and scenic journey.

Booking: Tickets can be purchased at train stations or online. While advanced booking is recommended for the Alfa Pendular service, regional trains usually have flexible ticketing options.

Regional Lines: Regional trains connect various towns and cities, making it easy to explore the country at a leisurely pace. The scenic route along the coast from Lisbon to Cascais is particularly popular among tourists.

Public Transport

Metro: Both Spain and Portugal have efficient metro systems in their major cities.

- **Madrid Metro**: One of the largest metro systems in Europe, it offers extensive coverage throughout the city and is known for its punctuality and cleanliness. Tickets can be purchased at stations, and multiple travel options are available, including single tickets, 10-ride tickets, and daily passes.

- **Lisbon Metro**: Lisbon's metro system is smaller but efficient, connecting the city's main districts. It is easy to navigate, and tickets can also be purchased at machines in stations. The **Lisbon Card** offers unlimited travel on public transport and discounts at attractions.

Buses: Buses complement metro services in both countries, providing access to areas not served by trains or metros.

- **Spain**: Intercity bus services, like ALSA, connect cities across Spain, offering affordable fares and frequent departures. City buses provide transportation within urban areas.
- **Portugal**: In Portugal, city buses are a convenient way to get around cities like Lisbon and Porto. Intercity buses also connect smaller towns and cities, with companies like Rede Expressos providing reliable services.

Taxis: Taxis are widely available in both Spain and Portugal, providing convenient door-to-door transportation.

- **Spain**: Taxis can be hailed on the street or booked via phone or apps like Uber. Taxi fares are metered, and additional charges may apply for luggage or late-night rides.
- **Portugal**: Taxis in Portugal are also metered, and ride-sharing apps like Uber and Bolt are popular in cities like Lisbon and Porto, offering competitive rates and easy booking.

Renting a Car

Renting a car can be an excellent way to explore Spain and Portugal, especially if you plan to visit rural areas or regions not easily accessible by public transport.

Car Rental Companies: Major international car rental companies operate in both countries, including Hertz, Avis, and Europcar. Local companies also offer competitive rates and services.

Driving License: A valid driver's license is required, and an International Driving Permit (IDP) is recommended, especially for non-EU travelers.

Road Conditions: Both Spain and Portugal have well-maintained road networks. Major highways (autopistas in Spain, autoestradas in Portugal) are typically toll roads, while secondary roads may be less congested but require more time for travel.

Driving Rules:

Drive on the right side of the road.

Seat belts are mandatory for all passengers.

Using a mobile phone while driving is prohibited unless hands-free.

Speed limits are usually 120 km/h (75 mph) on highways, 90 km/h (56 mph) on secondary roads, and 50 km/h (31 mph) in urban areas.

Parking: Parking can be challenging in major cities. Look for public parking garages or designated parking areas. Pay attention to signage indicating parking regulations, as fines can be hefty.

Traveling around Spain and Portugal is made easy with a variety of transportation options. Whether you choose to explore the bustling cities by metro and bus, take advantage of the efficient train systems, or enjoy the freedom of renting a car, you'll find that navigating these beautiful countries is a straightforward and enjoyable experience. With proper planning and knowledge of local transport systems, you can maximize your adventures and make the most of your time in Spain and Portugal.

Accommodation Options

Spain and Portugal offer a diverse range of accommodation options to suit every traveler's budget and preferences. From luxurious hotels to unique rural stays, finding the perfect place to rest after a day of exploring is key to an enjoyable trip. Here's a comprehensive overview of the various accommodation options available in these vibrant countries.

Luxury Hotels

For those seeking the ultimate in comfort and service, Spain and Portugal are home to numerous luxury hotels that provide world-class amenities, exquisite dining options, and exceptional hospitality.

- **Spain**:

The Ritz Madrid: This iconic hotel combines luxury with history, offering opulent rooms and a prime location near cultural attractions like the Prado Museum and Retiro Park.

Hotel Alfonso XIII, Seville: Known for its stunning Moorish architecture, this hotel provides a lavish stay in the heart of Seville, close to major attractions like the Alcázar and Seville Cathedral.

- **Portugal**:

Pestana Palace Lisboa: A UNESCO World Heritage Site, this hotel is set in a restored 19th-century palace and boasts beautiful gardens, luxurious rooms, and a spa.

The Yeatman, Porto: Located in the historic Vila Nova de Gaia, this hotel is famous for its stunning views of Porto and offers a world-class wine cellar and gourmet dining.

Boutique Stays

Boutique hotels are ideal for travelers looking for unique accommodations with personalized service and character. These properties often reflect the local culture and aesthetics.

Spain:

Hotel Casa Fuster, Barcelona: A modernist masterpiece designed by architect Lluís Domènech i Montaner, this boutique hotel features elegant rooms, a rooftop terrace, and is located near Passeig de Gràcia.

Hotel Palacio de Villapanés, Seville: Set in a restored 18th-century palace, this boutique hotel offers beautifully decorated rooms, a tranquil courtyard, and an excellent location near the historic center.

- **Portugal**:

Memmo Alfama Hotel, Lisbon: Nestled in the Alfama district, this stylish boutique hotel features contemporary design, stunning views of the Tagus River, and a rooftop pool.

Torel Avantgarde, Porto: This art-themed boutique hotel is situated in a historic building and showcases unique artwork, luxurious rooms, and beautiful gardens overlooking the Douro River.

Hostels

For budget-conscious travelers, hostels provide affordable accommodations, often with a vibrant social atmosphere. They are ideal for meeting fellow travelers and sharing experiences.

- **Spain**:

Kabul Party Hostel, Barcelona: Located in the lively Gothic Quarter, this hostel is known for its fun atmosphere, organized events, and proximity to nightlife.

The Hat, Madrid: A stylish hostel with a rooftop terrace and a bar, offering both dormitory and private room options in the heart of the city.

Portugal:

Lisbon Destination Hostel: Situated in the historic Rossio train station, this hostel features a mix of dorms and private rooms, as well as a vibrant common area for socializing.

Gallery Hostel, Porto: An artistic hostel that showcases local artists' work, offering a cozy atmosphere and a variety of room options.

Airbnb

Airbnb offers a wide range of accommodations, from private rooms to entire homes, allowing travelers to experience local living and often find unique places to stay.

- **Spain**:

Search for charming apartments in historic neighborhoods like the **Barrio Gótico** in Barcelona or the **Malasaña** district in Madrid. Many listings feature local decor and offer easy access to public transport and attractions.

- **Portugal**:

Consider staying in traditional **azulejo-tiled** houses in Lisbon or coastal villas in the Algarve. Airbnb also has listings for unique stays, such as former wine cellars or restored palaces.

Unique Stay

For a truly distinctive experience, consider staying in a **parador**, a **rural tourism** accommodation, or a **farmhouse**. These options provide insight into local culture and history.

Paradores:

These government-owned hotels are typically located in historic buildings, such as castles, monasteries, or palaces. They offer luxury accommodations with a unique cultural experience.

Examples include **Parador de Granada**, set within the Alhambra complex, and **Parador de Ronda**, perched on a cliff overlooking a gorge in Andalusia.

Rural Tourism:

Both Spain and Portugal have embraced rural tourism, offering accommodations in scenic countryside locations. These stays often include activities like hiking, wine tasting, and farm tours. Look for **casa rurals** in Spain or **agroturismos** in Portugal.

Farmhouses:

Staying in a farmhouse allows visitors to experience rural life firsthand. Many farmhouses offer cozy accommodations, home-cooked meals, and opportunities to engage in activities like olive oil production or grape harvesting. Look for listings in the **Alentejo** region in Portugal or **La Rioja** in Spain.

Spain and Portugal cater to a variety of accommodation preferences, from luxurious hotels and charming boutique stays to budget-friendly hostels and unique rural experiences. With such diverse options, travelers can find the perfect base for their adventures, ensuring a memorable trip filled with comfort, culture, and local charm.

Cuisine and Dining Tips

Spain and Portugal boast rich culinary traditions that reflect their diverse landscapes, cultures, and histories.

From vibrant tapas to hearty seafood dishes, exploring the local cuisine is an essential part of any visit. Here's a comprehensive overview of the culinary delights in these two countries, along with dining tips and recommendations for the best restaurants and local eateries.

Spanish Cuisine

Spanish cuisine is characterized by its bold flavors, fresh ingredients, and communal dining culture. Here are some key dishes you should try:

- **Tapas**: These small plates are perfect for sharing and sampling a variety of flavors. Tapas can include anything from **patatas bravas** (fried potatoes with spicy tomato sauce) and **gambas al ajillo** (garlic shrimp) to **chorizo al vino** (chorizo in wine). Bars and restaurants often have their own specialties, so be sure to try different places.
- **Paella**: Originating from the Valencia region, paella is a beloved rice dish that typically includes saffron, vegetables, and various proteins such as chicken, rabbit, or seafood. The traditional **paella valenciana** is made with chicken and rabbit, while **paella de mariscos** features an assortment of fresh seafood. It's

often served family-style and is a must-try when in Spain.

- **Jamón**: Spanish ham, particularly **jamón ibérico** and **jamón serrano,** is world-renowned. These hams are cured for several months and served thinly sliced. Enjoy them as part of a charcuterie board or as a tapa, accompanied by a glass of wine.

Dining Tip: When dining in Spain, meal times are typically later than in many other countries. Lunch usually starts around 2 PM, and dinner can begin as late as 9 PM or 10 PM. Embrace the local culture by adjusting your schedule to enjoy meals at traditional times.

Portuguese Cuisine

Portuguese cuisine is hearty and flavorful, emphasizing seafood, rich sauces, and delicious pastries. Here are some iconic dishes to seek out:

Bacalhau: Codfish is a staple in Portuguese cuisine, with numerous preparation methods. The phrase "there are a thousand ways to prepare bacalhau" speaks to its versatility. Popular dishes include **bacalhau à brás** (shredded cod with potatoes and eggs) and **bacalhau com natas** (cod with cream).

Pastel de Nata: These iconic Portuguese custard tarts are a must-try. With a crispy, flaky crust and a creamy filling, pastéis de nata are often enjoyed with a sprinkle of cinnamon and powdered sugar. Head to **Pastéis de Belém** in Lisbon for some of the best.

Francesinha: This hearty sandwich from Porto is a true comfort food. It consists of layers of cured meats, steak, and sausage, all covered in a rich tomato and beer sauce, often served with French fries. It's a filling dish perfect for cold days.

Dining Tip: In Portugal, it's common to see **petiscos**, similar to Spanish tapas, on menus. These small plates are ideal for sharing and trying a variety of local specialties. Don't hesitate to ask for recommendations from your server.

Best Restaurants and Local Eateries

When exploring the culinary scene in Spain and Portugal, consider visiting both acclaimed restaurants and local eateries for an authentic experience.

Spain:

El Celler de Can Roca (Girona): This three-Michelin-star restaurant, run by the Roca brothers, offers innovative Catalan cuisine in a beautiful setting. Reservations are essential, as it is one of the top dining destinations in the world.

Bar Tomate (Madrid): A stylish spot known for its Mediterranean-inspired dishes and vibrant atmosphere. It's a great place to enjoy tapas and fresh seasonal ingredients.

Mercat de Sant Josep de la Boqueria (Barcelona): This famous market is a must-visit for food lovers. You'll find fresh produce, meats, and seafood, as well as stalls serving delicious tapas.

Portugal:

Time Out Market (Lisbon): This food hall features a curated selection of the city's best chefs and restaurants, offering a diverse range of local dishes in a lively atmosphere.

Cervejaria Ramiro (Lisbon): Renowned for its fresh seafood, this casual eatery is famous for its garlic shrimp, crab, and beer. Be prepared for a wait, as it's popular among locals and tourists alike.

Taberna da Ribeira (Porto): This cozy tavern serves traditional Portuguese dishes in a warm atmosphere. It's a great place to sample local wines alongside hearty meals.

Wine and Spirits

Both Spain and Portugal have rich wine traditions, producing a variety of acclaimed wines that perfectly complement their culinary offerings.

Spanish Wines: Spain is home to several renowned wine regions, including **Rioja**, **Ribera del Duero**, and **Priorat**. Look for red wines made from **Tempranillo** and **Garnacha** grapes, as well as excellent white wines like **Albariño** from the Rías Baixas region. Wine tasting tours are popular in many regions, providing insights into the winemaking process.

Port Wine: Originating from the Douro Valley in northern Portugal, Port wine is a fortified wine that comes in various styles, including ruby, tawny, and vintage. A visit to the wine cellars in Porto is a must for tasting and learning about the production process. Pair Port with cheese or chocolate for a delightful dessert experience.

Vinho Verde: This unique wine from Portugal's Minho region is known for its lightness and refreshing qualities. Often slightly effervescent, Vinho Verde is perfect for warm weather and pairs well with seafood and light dishes.

Dining Tip: When dining, ask for a wine recommendation based on your meal. Most restaurants will have knowledgeable staff who can suggest the perfect pairing to enhance your dining experience.

Exploring the culinary landscapes of Spain and Portugal is a journey in itself, offering a delightful blend of flavors, traditions, and experiences. From savoring tapas and bacalhau to indulging in pastéis de nata and local wines, food lovers will find endless opportunities to taste the rich cultures of these two captivating countries. Enjoy your culinary adventure!

CHAPTER 5

Suggested Itineraries

Traveling through Spain and Portugal can be an enriching experience, allowing you to immerse yourself in vibrant cultures, stunning landscapes, and delicious cuisines. Here are some suggested itineraries to help you make the most of your trip, whether you're interested in a classic tour, a family-friendly adventure, or a combined experience of both countries.

Classic Spain in 10 Days

This itinerary highlights the cultural and historical gems of Spain, offering a blend of art, architecture, and gastronomy.

Day 1-3: Madrid

Day 1: Arrive in Madrid. Explore the **Prado Museum** and **Retiro Park**. Enjoy dinner at a local tapas bar in the **La Latina** neighborhood.

Day 2: Visit the **Royal Palace** and the **Thyssen-Bornemisza Museum**. Take a stroll through **Plaza Mayor** and sample traditional churros with chocolate at **Chocolatería San Ginés**.

Day 3: Day trip to **Toledo** (about 30 minutes by train). Discover the historic city's Moorish architecture, including the **Toledo Cathedral** and **Alcázar**.

Day 4-5: Seville

Day 4: Travel to Seville (about 2.5 hours by train). Visit the **Seville Cathedral** and **La Giralda** tower, followed by an evening flamenco show in **Barrio Santa Cruz**.

Day 5: Explore the **Alcázar of Seville** and **Plaza de España**. Enjoy a leisurely walk along the **Guadalquivir River** and dine at a local restaurant.

Day 6-7: Granada

Day 6: Head to Granada (approximately 3 hours by train or bus). Visit the **Alhambra** and stroll through the **Generalife Gardens**.

Day 7: Explore the **Albayzín** neighborhood, known for its narrow winding streets and views of the Alhambra. Consider a visit to a traditional **hamam** (Arab bath).

Day 8-10: Barcelona

Day 8: Travel to Barcelona (about 6.5 hours by train). Spend the afternoon visiting **Park Güell** and **La Sagrada Familia**.

Day 9: Explore the **Gothic Quarter** and visit **Casa Batlló** and **Casa Milà** (La Pedrera). Enjoy dinner in the **El Born** district.

Day 10: Relax at the beach or visit **Montjuïc** for panoramic views and attractions like the **Magic Fountain**.

The Best of Portugal in 7 Days

This itinerary captures the essence of Portugal, from bustling cities to serene landscapes.

Day 1-3: Lisbon

Day 1: Arrive in Lisbon. Explore the **Alfama District**, visit the **São Jorge Castle**, and enjoy dinner at a local restaurant.

Day 2: Visit the **Belém Tower** and **Jerónimos Monastery**. Indulge in **pastéis de nata** at **Pastéis de Belém**. In the evening, enjoy fado music in a traditional tavern.

- **Day 3**: Day trip to **Sintra** to visit the **Pena Palace** and **Quinta da Regaleira**. Return to Lisbon for the night.

Day 4-5: Porto

- **Day 4**: Travel to Porto (about 3 hours by train). Explore the **Ribeira District**, visit **Livraria Lello**, and enjoy a port wine tasting at one of the wine cellars.
- **Day 5**: Visit **São Bento Station**, the **Clérigos Tower**, and the **Palácio da Bolsa**. Take a boat tour along the Douro River for stunning views of the city.

Day 6: Douro Valley

- **Day 6**: Take a day trip to the **Douro Valley**, known for its vineyards and breathtaking landscapes. Consider a river cruise or wine tour at local quintas (wineries).

Day 7: Algarve

- **Day 7**: Travel to the **Algarve** (approximately 5 hours by train or bus). Relax on the beautiful beaches of Lagos or Albufeira, and explore the stunning cliffs of Ponta da Piedade.

Combined Spain & Portugal Tour (14 Days)

For travelers wishing to experience both countries, this itinerary offers a comprehensive tour.

Day 1-5: Madrid, Toledo, Seville

- **Day 1**: Arrive in Madrid. Explore the main attractions.
- **Day 2**: Visit Toledo for the day.
- **Day 3**: Travel to Seville and explore its landmarks.
- **Day 4**: Continue exploring Seville, including a flamenco show.
- **Day 5**: Day trip to Córdoba (about 45 minutes from Seville) to see the **Mezquita**.

Day 6-9: Lisbon, Sintra, Porto

- **Day 6**: Travel to Lisbon (about 1.5 hours by flight or train). Explore Lisbon's neighborhoods.
- **Day 7**: Visit Sintra.
- **Day 8**: Travel to Porto. Explore the Ribeira District.
- **Day 9**: Enjoy a day in Porto, including wine tasting.

Day 10-14: Barcelona, Valencia

- **Day 10**: Fly to Barcelona. Explore the city's highlights.
- **Day 11**: Continue exploring Barcelona, including the Gothic Quarter.
- **Day 12**: Travel to Valencia (about 3.5 hours by train). Visit the City of Arts and Sciences.
- **Day 13**: Enjoy Valencia's beaches and the historic center.
- **Day 14**: Depart from Valencia or return to Barcelona for your flight home.

Family-Friendly Spain & Portugal

Traveling with kids? Here's an itinerary filled with family-friendly activities that engage and entertain.

Spain

- **Madrid**: Visit **Parque de Atracciones** (amusement park) and the **Madrid Zoo Aquarium**.
- **Barcelona**: Explore **CosmoCaixa**, the science museum, and enjoy a day at the beach at **Barceloneta**.
- **Seville**: Take a horse-drawn carriage ride and visit the **Isla Mágica** theme park.

Portugal

- **Lisbon**: Explore the **Lisbon Oceanarium** and take a tram ride on the historic **Tram 28**.
- **Porto**: Visit the **World of Discoveries** museum and take a boat ride on the Douro River.
- **Algarve**: Spend a day at one of the region's family-friendly beaches, such as **Praia da Rocha**, and visit **Zoomarine**, a marine park.

Adventure and Outdoor Lovers

For those who seek outdoor adventures, Spain and Portugal offer breathtaking landscapes and activities for nature enthusiasts.

Spain

- **Hiking**: Explore the **Picos de Europa** National Park for stunning mountain trails or the **Camino de Santiago**, a famous pilgrimage route.
- **Beaches**: Relax on the beaches of **Costa Brava** or **Costa del Sol**, known for their picturesque shores and crystal-clear waters.

Portugal

Hiking: Discover the **Rota Vicentina**, a network of walking trails along the Alentejo coast, or hike in the **Arrábida Natural Park** near Lisbon.

Beaches: The Algarve region offers beautiful beaches, such as **Praia da Marinha** and **Ponta da Piedade**, ideal for sunbathing, swimming, and water sports.

These suggested itineraries cater to various interests, ensuring that travelers can explore the best of Spain and Portugal according to their preferences and time constraints. Whether you're looking for a classic cultural experience, family-friendly fun, or outdoor adventures, there's something for everyone in these captivating countries. Enjoy your journey!

CHAPTER 6

Cultural Insights

Spain and Portugal are rich in cultural traditions and vibrant customs that reflect their history, geography, and the diverse influences that have shaped them over centuries. Understanding these cultural insights will enhance your travel experience and deepen your appreciation for the people and places you encounter.

Spanish Culture and Traditions

Spanish culture is a blend of various regional identities, each with its own distinct customs and traditions. The country is known for its lively social atmosphere, emphasis on family, and celebration of life through art, music, and festivals. Here are some key elements of Spanish culture:

Flamenco: This passionate art form combines singing, guitar playing, dance, and handclaps, originating from the Andalusian gypsy community. Flamenco performances often take place in intimate venues known as **tablaos**, where you can experience the raw emotion and skill of the artists. The dance is characterized by intricate footwork and expressive movements, making it a captivating experience.

Bullfighting: While controversial, bullfighting has deep roots in Spanish tradition and is often regarded as a form of art. The **corrida de toros** (bullfight) typically involves a series of choreographed events where a matador confronts a bull in a ring. Major bullfighting events are held in cities like Seville, Madrid, and Pamplona. However, it's essential to approach this cultural practice with an understanding of the differing opinions surrounding it.

Siestas: The Spanish tradition of taking a midday break, known as a siesta, is a practice deeply ingrained in the culture. Typically observed in the early afternoon, businesses may close for a few hours, allowing locals to rest and recharge. This cultural practice reflects the emphasis on a balanced lifestyle, prioritizing family time and relaxation.

Fiestas: Spaniards love to celebrate, and various fiestas take place throughout the year. These festivals can range from religious observances to local fairs and cultural events. They often include music, dancing, food, and vibrant parades, bringing communities together to honor their traditions.

Spain is home to numerous festivals that showcase its cultural richness and diversity. Here are some of the most iconic festivals worth experiencing:

- **La Tomatina** (Buñol): Held annually on the last Wednesday of August, La Tomatina is a unique festival where participants engage in a massive tomato fight. Thousands of people gather in the town of Buñol to throw overripe tomatoes at each other, creating a lively and messy atmosphere. The event is celebrated for its fun and playful spirit.
- **Feria de Abril** (Seville): This famous spring fair takes place two weeks after Easter and lasts for a week. The streets of Seville come alive with colorful tents, flamenco music, traditional dances, and delicious food. Locals dress in traditional attire, and activities include horse

rides, bullfighting, and various games. The
Feria is a time for celebration, socializing, and
showcasing Andalusian culture.

- **Semana Santa** (Holy Week): Celebrated in the
  week leading up to Easter, Semana Santa is one
  of the most significant religious festivals in
  Spain. Cities like Seville, Málaga, and Granada
  host elaborate processions featuring religious
  brotherhoods carrying beautifully adorned pasos
  (floats). Participants often wear traditional robes
  and carry candles, creating a solemn yet vibrant
  atmosphere. The processions are accompanied
  by music, and the event attracts both locals and
  tourists who wish to witness this deeply rooted
  tradition.

Spain's cultural landscape is characterized by its
diversity, rich traditions, and vibrant celebrations.
From the passionate rhythms of flamenco to the lively
atmosphere of local fiestas, there's always something
captivating to discover. Embracing these cultural
insights will not only enhance your travel experience
but also foster a deeper connection with the people and
places you encounter along your journey.

Portuguese Culture and Traditions

Portugal boasts a rich cultural heritage shaped by its history, geography, and diverse influences. The country's traditions reflect a unique blend of customs, music, art, and cuisine, making it a fascinating destination for travelers. Here's an overview of some key elements of Portuguese culture, along with notable festivals that showcase its vibrant spirit.

Portuguese Culture and Traditions

Fado Music: Fado is an iconic music genre that embodies the soul of Portuguese culture. Characterized by its mournful melodies and poignant lyrics, Fado often expresses themes of longing, nostalgia, and the complexities of life (known as **saudade**). Typically performed in intimate venues, Fado singers (fadistas) are accompanied by Portuguese guitars and other instruments. The most famous Fado scene is found in the **Alfama district** of Lisbon, where traditional taverns host live performances, allowing visitors to experience the deep emotional connection embedded in this art form.

Portuguese Tiles (Azulejos): Azulejos are decorative ceramic tiles that have become a hallmark of Portuguese architecture and design. These intricate tiles, often painted in vibrant colors and patterns, adorn everything from historical buildings to modern homes. They are commonly used in facades, interior walls, and even public spaces like train stations. The history of azulejos dates back to the Moorish influence in the 15th century, and their designs often depict scenes from nature, mythology, or everyday life, serving as both artistic expression and storytelling.

Cork Industry: Portugal is the largest producer of cork in the world, contributing significantly to the country's economy and heritage. The cork oak tree, which can live for over 200 years, is harvested every nine years without harming the tree, making cork an environmentally friendly material. Cork is used in various products, from wine stoppers to flooring and fashion items. Visitors can learn about this unique industry by visiting cork farms and museums, where they can see the harvesting process and the versatility of cork products.

Portugal is known for its lively festivals that celebrate its traditions, religion, and community spirit. Here are some notable festivals worth experiencing:

Santo António (Lisbon): Celebrated on June 13th, Santo António is the patron saint of Lisbon, and his feast day is marked by vibrant street parties, parades, and processions. The city comes alive with music, dancing, and the aroma of grilled sardines wafting through the streets. People decorate their homes with colorful garlands and participate in the traditional custom of "santo António's matchmaking," where single individuals pray for the saint's assistance in finding a partner.

São João (Porto): Taking place on the night of June 23rd, São João is one of Porto's most famous and lively festivals. The celebration begins with a parade featuring traditional costumes and music, followed by fireworks over the Douro River. Participants often carry plastic hammers to playfully hit each other on the head and release lanterns into the night sky. The festivities culminate in street parties, where people enjoy traditional foods and drinks, creating a joyous and festive atmosphere throughout the city.

Carnival: Carnival is celebrated throughout Portugal, with each region showcasing its unique traditions and customs. The most famous Carnival celebrations take place in **Madeira** and **Loulé** (in the Algarve). The festivities typically include colorful parades, elaborate costumes, music, and dancing, creating a lively atmosphere. The celebrations often culminate in the days leading up to Lent, with vibrant events that encourage revelry and joy before the solemn season.

Portugal's culture is deeply rooted in its traditions, music, and arts, which continue to thrive and evolve. From the heartfelt strains of Fado to the beauty of azulejos and the lively atmosphere of local festivals, experiencing Portuguese culture will enrich your travel journey. Engaging with these customs not only fosters a deeper understanding of the people and their history but also creates lasting memories that capture the essence of Portugal.

Language Basics

Understanding some basic phrases in Spanish and Portuguese can significantly enhance your travel experience in Spain and Portugal. Even if you're not fluent, making an effort to communicate in the local language is often appreciated by residents. Here's a guide to essential phrases and useful expressions to help you navigate your journey.

Essential Spanish Phrases

Greetings and Basic Interactions:

- **Hola** – Hello
- **Buenos días** – Good morning
- **Buenas tardes** – Good afternoon
- **Buenas noches** – Good evening / Good night
- **¿Cómo estás?** – How are you?
- **Estoy bien, gracias** – I'm fine, thank you.
- **¿Y tú?** – And you?

Common Questions:

- **¿Qué tal?** – How's it going?
- **¿Dónde está...?** – Where is...?
- **¿Cuánto cuesta?** – How much does it cost?
- **¿Habla inglés?** – Do you speak English?

- **¿Puede ayudarme?** – Can you help me?
- **¿Cuál es tu nombre?** – What is your name?

Useful Expressions:

- **Por favor** – Please
- **Gracias** – Thank you
- **De nada** – You're welcome
- **Lo siento** – I'm sorry
- **Sí** – Yes
- **No** – No
- **Tal vez** – Maybe

Essential Portuguese Phrases

Greetings and Basic Interactions:

- **Olá** – Hello
- **Bom dia** – Good morning
- **Boa tarde** – Good afternoon
- **Boa noite** – Good evening / Good night
- **Como você está?** – How are you?
- **Estou bem, obrigado/a** – I'm fine, thank you. (Use "obrigado" if you are male and "obrigada" if you are female.)
- **E você?** – And you?

Common Questions:

- **Tudo bem?** – Is everything good?
- **Onde está...?** – Where is...?
- **Quanto custa?** – How much does it cost?
- **Você fala inglês?** – Do you speak English?
- **Pode me ajudar?** – Can you help me?
- **Qual é o seu nome?** – What is your name?

Useful Expressions:

- **Por favor** – Please
- **Obrigado/a** – Thank you (same gender rules apply)
- **De nada** – You're welcome
- **Desculpe** – I'm sorry
- **Sim** – Yes
- **Não** – No
- **Talvez** – Maybe

Useful Expressions for Travelers

In addition to basic phrases, here are some useful expressions that can help you while traveling:

Dining Out:

- **La cuenta, por favor.** (Spanish) / **A conta, por favor.** (Portuguese) – The bill, please.

- **Una mesa para dos, por favor.** (Spanish) / **Uma mesa para dois, por favor.** (Portuguese) – A table for two, please.
- **Estoy buscando un restaurante.** (Spanish) / **Estou procurando um restaurante.** (Portuguese) – I'm looking for a restaurant.

Navigating:

- **¿Dónde está la estación de tren?** (Spanish) / **Onde fica a estação de trem?** (Portuguese) – Where is the train station?
- **¿Cómo llego a...?** (Spanish) / **Como chego a...?** (Portuguese) – How do I get to...?

Shopping:

- **¿Tienen esto en otro tamaño/color?** (Spanish) / **Você tem isso em outro tamanho/cor?** (Portuguese) – Do you have this in another size/color?
- **¿Puedo probarme esto?** (Spanish) / **Posso experimentar isso?** (Portuguese) – Can I try this on?

Emergency Situations:

- **¡Ayuda!** – Help!

- **Necesito un médico.** (Spanish) / **Preciso de um médico.** (Portuguese) – I need a doctor.
- **Llama a la policía.** (Spanish) / **Chame a polícia.** (Portuguese) – Call the police.

Familiarizing yourself with these essential phrases can help you engage with locals and navigate daily interactions in Spain and Portugal. Even a small effort to communicate in their languages can lead to warmer responses and a richer travel experience. Enjoy your journey!

CHAPTER 7

Outdoor Adventures

Spain and Portugal offer a stunning array of outdoor adventures, particularly along their picturesque coastlines and breathtaking beaches. From the vibrant shores of the Mediterranean to the rugged cliffs of the Atlantic, both countries boast some of the best beach destinations in Europe. Whether you seek relaxation, water sports, or scenic hikes, here's a comprehensive look at the top beach destinations in Spain and Portugal.

Beaches and Coastlines

The beaches of Spain and Portugal are not just places to soak up the sun; they are gateways to various outdoor activities, scenic landscapes, and unique experiences. With their diverse coastlines, travelers can find everything from family-friendly beaches to hidden coves perfect for snorkeling and diving.

Best Beaches in Spain

Costa Brava:

Description: Known for its rugged coastline and charming villages, Costa Brava offers crystal-clear waters, hidden coves, and beautiful sandy beaches. The region is a favorite among locals and tourists alike.

Highlights:

Platja de Calella: A long, sandy beach popular for sunbathing and water sports. The beach is surrounded by scenic cliffs and boasts clear waters.

Cala Montjoi: A secluded cove famous for its natural beauty, perfect for swimming and snorkeling.

Tossa de Mar: Features a stunning medieval castle overlooking the beach, combining history with beach fun.

Costa del Sol:

Description: Famous for its sunny weather, Costa del Sol is a top destination for beach lovers. The coastline is dotted with resorts, restaurants, and vibrant nightlife.

Playa de la Malagueta: A lively urban beach located in Málaga, ideal for enjoying local cuisine at beachside chiringuitos (restaurants).

Nerja: Known for its stunning Balcon de Europa viewpoint and beautiful beaches like Playa de Burriana, perfect for families and water sports enthusiasts.

Puerto Banús: A glamorous beach area popular with celebrities, featuring luxurious yachts and upscale boutiques.

Canary Islands:

Description: Located off the northwest coast of Africa, the Canary Islands offer diverse landscapes, including volcanic beaches, lush forests, and dramatic cliffs.

Playa de las Teresitas (Tenerife): An artificial beach with golden sand and calm waters, perfect for families and sunbathing.

Playa del Inglés (Gran Canaria): A bustling beach with a vibrant atmosphere, ideal for water sports and nightlife.

Papagayo Beaches (Lanzarote): A series of pristine beaches with clear waters and stunning landscapes, perfect for swimming and snorkeling.

Best Beaches in Portugal

- **Algarve**:

Description: The Algarve is renowned for its stunning cliffs, golden sandy beaches, and clear waters. It is a top destination for sun-seekers and adventure lovers alike.

Praia da Marinha: Frequently ranked among the best beaches in the world, known for its dramatic cliffs and crystal-clear waters, perfect for snorkeling and diving.

Praia do Amado: A popular beach for surfing, with consistent waves and surf schools for beginners.

Praia de Lagos: Features stunning rock formations and hidden caves, ideal for kayaking and exploring the coastline.

Costa Vicentina:

Description: Part of the Southwest Alentejo and Vicentine Coast Natural Park, this region is known for its untouched beauty and rugged landscapes.

Amado Beach: A popular surfing spot with a relaxed atmosphere and breathtaking cliffs.

Arrifana Beach: Nestled between steep cliffs, this beach is perfect for swimming, surfing, and enjoying scenic hikes along the coastline.

Castelejo Beach: A wild, unspoiled beach great for sunbathing and long walks, with dramatic cliffs and stunning sunsets.

- **Madeira**:

Description: Known for its lush landscapes and volcanic beaches, Madeira offers unique beach experiences, blending nature with outdoor adventures.

Praia Formosa: The largest public beach on the island, featuring a mix of pebbles and sand, with stunning views of the surrounding mountains.

Praia de Calheta: An artificial beach with golden sand imported from Morocco, perfect for families and water sports.

Ponta de São Lourenço: While not a traditional beach, this natural reserve offers stunning coastal views and hiking trails along dramatic cliffs.

Spain and Portugal's coastlines are filled with breathtaking beaches that cater to all types of travelers. From the sun-kissed shores of the Costa del Sol to the rugged beauty of the Algarve, outdoor adventures await you. Whether you prefer lounging on the beach, engaging in water sports, or exploring scenic trails, these coastal destinations offer unforgettable experiences in the great outdoors.

Hiking and Nature

Both Spain and Portugal are blessed with stunning natural landscapes that offer a diverse range of hiking opportunities. From well-trodden pilgrimage paths to breathtaking mountain ranges and lush national parks, outdoor enthusiasts will find plenty to explore. Here's a comprehensive look at some of the best hiking destinations in both countries.

Hiking in Spain

Camino de Santiago:

Overview: The Camino de Santiago, or the Way of St. James, is one of the most famous pilgrimage routes in the world. It culminates at the Cathedral of Santiago de Compostela in Galicia, where the remains of Saint James are believed to be buried.

Routes: There are several routes, with the most popular being the **Camino Francés**, which starts in Saint-Jean-Pied-de-Port, France, and stretches about 800 kilometers (500 miles) across northern Spain. Other notable routes include the **Camino del Norte** along the northern coast and the **Via de la Plata** in the south.

Experience: Hikers can enjoy stunning landscapes, charming villages, and a rich cultural heritage. Along the way, travelers often meet fellow pilgrims and experience the camaraderie that characterizes the journey.

Picos de Europa:

Overview: Located in northern Spain, the Picos de Europa National Park is known for its dramatic limestone peaks, deep gorges, and lush valleys. It is a paradise for hikers and nature lovers.

Cares Gorge (Ruta del Cares): This iconic hike follows a narrow path carved into the cliffs, offering breathtaking views of the gorge and the surrounding mountains. The route stretches about 12 kilometers (7.5 miles) one way.

Naranjo de Bulnes: A challenging ascent to the summit of this iconic peak rewards hikers with panoramic views of the Picos de Europa.

Fuente Dé: Take a cable car to the top for stunning views and access to several hiking trails.

Pyrenees:

Overview: The Pyrenees form a natural border between Spain and France, offering a diverse range of hiking opportunities, from easy day hikes to multi-day treks.

Ordesa y Monte Perdido National Park: Known for its dramatic landscapes, this park features stunning valleys, waterfalls, and diverse wildlife. The **Ordesa**

Valley hike is particularly popular, showcasing breathtaking views.

GR10 Trail: This long-distance trail runs along the French side of the Pyrenees, but many sections extend into Spain, providing hikers with stunning mountain scenery and charming villages.

Aneto: The highest peak in the Pyrenees, Aneto is accessible via a challenging trek that rewards hikers with spectacular views of the surrounding mountain ranges.

Hiking in Portugal

Peneda-Gerês National Park:

Overview: Located in northern Portugal, Peneda-Gerês National Park is a UNESCO Biosphere Reserve known for its rugged terrain, diverse flora and fauna, and stunning landscapes.

Serradela Trail: A well-marked trail that takes hikers through beautiful valleys, alongside rivers, and to stunning viewpoints. The park is also home to ancient rock art and traditional villages.

Geres Waterfall Trail: A popular hike that leads to the stunning waterfalls of **Tahiti** and **Arado**, perfect for a refreshing dip in the natural pools.

Wildlife Watching: The park is home to diverse wildlife, including deer, wild boar, and the Iberian wolf.

Rota Vicentina:

Overview: Rota Vicentina is a network of walking trails along the southwestern coast of Portugal, showcasing stunning cliffs, pristine beaches, and charming fishing villages.

Fishermen's Trail: This coastal route follows the rugged coastline and offers breathtaking views of the Atlantic Ocean. Hikers can explore beautiful beaches and hidden coves while enjoying the region's diverse flora and fauna.

Historical Way: This inland route takes you through traditional villages, vineyards, and scenic countryside, providing a glimpse into local life.

Ecological Diversity: Rota Vicentina is rich in biodiversity, making it ideal for birdwatching and enjoying the region's natural beauty.

Madeira Levada Walks:

Overview: The island of Madeira is famous for its unique irrigation channels called **levadas**, which have been transformed into scenic walking paths. These trails offer stunning views of the island's lush landscapes and rugged cliffs.

Levada do Caldeirão Verde: A popular hike that follows a levada through lush forests to reach the breathtaking Caldeirão Verde waterfall.

Levada dos 25 Fontes: This trail takes hikers to the famous 25 Fountains, where numerous streams cascade down the cliffs into natural pools.

Pico Ruivo: The highest peak in Madeira offers challenging hikes that reward trekkers with panoramic views of the island and the surrounding ocean.

Spain and Portugal provide a wealth of outdoor adventures for hikers and nature enthusiasts. From the iconic Camino de Santiago to the stunning landscapes of the Picos de Europa and the unique levada walks of Madeira, both countries offer unforgettable experiences for those who appreciate the great outdoors. Whether you're a seasoned hiker or a casual walker, these trails provide opportunities to connect with nature and explore the beauty of the Iberian Peninsula.

Water Sports and Adventure Activities

Spain and Portugal are not only renowned for their picturesque coastlines and vibrant culture, but they also offer a plethora of thrilling water sports and adventure activities. From surfing the massive waves of Nazaré to exploring underwater landscapes through diving, both countries are perfect playgrounds for water enthusiasts. Here's a comprehensive overview of the top water sports and adventure activities available in Spain and Portugal.

Surfing in Portugal

Nazaré:

Overview: Nazaré is famous for its colossal waves, making it a premier destination for surfers worldwide. The underwater canyon off the coast creates conditions for some of the biggest surfable waves on the planet, attracting professional surfers to tackle its monstrous swells.

Praia do Norte: This beach is renowned for its gigantic waves, particularly during the winter months. The combination of the deep sea canyon and the beach break results in waves that can exceed 30 meters (98 feet) in height.

Big Wave Surfing: The area is famous for hosting international big wave competitions, drawing surfers and spectators from around the globe.

Surf Schools: For those looking to learn, several surf schools offer lessons tailored to different skill levels, making it accessible for beginners to experience the thrill of catching a wave.

Ericeira:

Overview: Recognized as a World Surfing Reserve, Ericeira boasts a variety of surf spots suitable for all levels, from beginners to seasoned pros.

Praia de Ribeira d'Ilhas: Known for its consistent surf conditions, this beach is a favorite among surfers and has hosted numerous national and international competitions.

Foz do Lizandro: This beach offers mellow waves, making it ideal for beginners and longboarders.

Surf Camps and Schools: Ericeira is home to many surf camps that provide lessons, equipment rental, and guided tours to various surf spots along the coastline.

Diving, Kayaking, and Sailing in Spain and Portugal

Diving:

Spain:

Canary Islands: Renowned for their clear waters and diverse marine life, the Canary Islands offer exceptional diving experiences. Popular dive sites include:

El Hierro: Known for its underwater volcanic formations and rich marine biodiversity.

Tenerife: Offers sites like the **Manta Ray Diving** and **Los Gigantes**, where divers can encounter a variety of marine species.

Catalonia: The **Medes Islands** Marine Reserve is a protected area famous for its clear waters, rich marine life, and underwater caves, perfect for divers of all skill levels.

Portugal:

Madeira: Known for its unique underwater ecosystems, Madeira offers diving experiences among colorful reefs, caves, and shipwrecks. Popular dive sites include:

Garajau Nature Reserve: A marine reserve with abundant fish life and the chance to see larger species like rays and moray eels.

Diving with Dolphins: Some operators offer unique experiences to dive or snorkel with wild dolphins in the surrounding waters.

Algarve: Known for its stunning underwater caves and cliffs, divers can explore sites like **Ponta da Piedade** and **Cape St. Vincent**.

Kayaking:

Overview: Kayaking is a popular way to explore the stunning coastlines of both Spain and Portugal. Many beaches and coastal areas offer rental services and guided tours.

Sea Kayaking in the Algarve: Explore hidden caves, secluded beaches, and stunning rock formations along the Algarve coast. Kayak tours often include visits to beautiful spots like **Benagil Cave** and **Ponta da Piedade**.

Kayaking in the Ria Formosa: This beautiful natural park in the Algarve is perfect for kayaking, where you can paddle through lagoons and spot diverse wildlife, including birds and marine life.

Costa Brava: Kayaking along the rugged coastline of Costa Brava allows paddlers to discover hidden coves, crystal-clear waters, and charming seaside villages.

Sailing:

Overview: With their beautiful coastlines and favorable winds, both Spain and Portugal are ideal destinations for sailing enthusiasts.

Sailing in Barcelona: The vibrant city offers sailing tours and yacht rentals, allowing visitors to explore the Mediterranean coast while enjoying stunning views of the city skyline and nearby beaches.

Sailing the Balearic Islands: Islands like **Ibiza** and **Mallorca** provide opportunities for island hopping, with clear waters perfect for anchoring and exploring secluded beaches.

Douro River Cruises: In Portugal, the Douro River offers unique sailing experiences, with wine tours available along the riverbanks, showcasing the famous vineyards of the Douro Valley.

Lisbon Sailing Tours: Experience the beauty of Lisbon from the water with sailing tours along the Tagus River, providing spectacular views of landmarks like the Belém Tower and the 25 de Abril Bridge.

Spain and Portugal offer an exciting array of water sports and adventure activities that cater to all levels of experience. From the legendary surf of Nazaré to the diverse underwater ecosystems of the Canary Islands and Madeira, outdoor enthusiasts will find countless opportunities for adventure. Whether you're a seasoned surfer, a curious diver, or an aspiring sailor, the waters of the Iberian Peninsula are waiting for you to explore!

CHAPTER 8

Culinary Experiences

Spain and Portugal are renowned for their rich culinary traditions and diverse flavors, making them premier destinations for food enthusiasts. From the vibrant atmosphere of tapas bars to the elegant vineyards of La Rioja and the bountiful seafood of the Atlantic coast, both countries offer a wide range of culinary experiences that celebrate local ingredients and regional specialties. Here's a comprehensive overview of the top culinary experiences to savor in Spain and Portugal.

Food and Drink Tours

Tapas Tours:

Overview: Tapas are small plates of food that can be enjoyed as appetizers or combined to create a full meal. Tapas culture is an integral part of Spanish social life, making a tapas tour an immersive culinary experience.

Seville:

Experience: In Seville, embark on a guided tapas tour through the historic Santa Cruz neighborhood. Sample traditional dishes like **salmorejo** (a cold tomato soup), **fried fish**, and **jamón ibérico** (Iberian ham) while visiting local bars and eateries.

Local Highlights: Don't miss the chance to try **flamenquín** (deep-fried meat rolls) and **churros** with chocolate at a traditional café.

Barcelona:

Experience: In Barcelona, explore the lively streets of the Gothic Quarter and El Born while tasting a variety of tapas, including **patatas bravas** (fried potatoes with spicy sauce), **pan con tomate** (toasted bread with tomato), and **seafood tapas**.

Local Highlights: Visit bustling markets like **Mercat de Sant Josep de la Boqueria** to sample fresh produce, cured meats, and local cheeses.

Madrid:

Experience: In Madrid, enjoy a tapas crawl through vibrant neighborhoods like La Latina, stopping at traditional bars to taste dishes like **tortilla española** (Spanish omelet) and **croquetas**.

Local Highlights: Try the famous **cocido madrileño**, a hearty chickpea-based stew, and finish your tour with a sweet treat, such as **tarta de Santiago** (almond cake).

Wine Tasting:

Overview: Spain and Portugal are home to some of the world's finest wines, with diverse regions producing unique varieties. Wine tasting tours offer an opportunity to explore vineyards, learn about winemaking, and sample exquisite wines.

La Rioja:

Experience: In La Rioja, visit prestigious wineries to learn about the region's rich viticulture and sample renowned red wines made primarily from the Tempranillo grape.

Local Highlights: Enjoy tastings paired with local delicacies such as **chorizo** and **cheeses**. Don't miss the chance to explore the picturesque town of **Haro**, known for its historic bodegas.

Douro Valley:

Experience: The Douro Valley, a UNESCO World Heritage site, is famous for its terraced vineyards and port wine production. Take a river cruise or guided tour through the valley, stopping at wineries for tastings.

Local Highlights: Sample port wines along with traditional Portuguese dishes, such as **bacalhau à Brás** (codfish) and **pastéis de nata** (custard tarts). Enjoy the stunning views of the river and vineyards from the terraces.

Seafood Experiences

Galicia:

Overview: Known for its rugged coastline and abundant seafood, Galicia is a paradise for seafood lovers. The region's fishing tradition ensures the freshest catches are available, with many dishes reflecting local culinary heritage.

Experience: Explore the coastal towns of Santiago de Compostela, A Coruña, and Vigo, indulging in seafood specialties such as **pulpo a la gallega** (Galician-style octopus), **empanada** (savory pie), and **percebes** (goose barnacles).

Local Highlights: Visit local markets to experience the lively atmosphere and purchase fresh seafood.

Participate in a cooking class to learn how to prepare traditional Galician dishes.

Algarve:

Overview: The Algarve region of Portugal is celebrated for its stunning beaches and fresh seafood. Its fishing villages and coastal towns offer a variety of seafood dining experiences.

Experience: Enjoy seafood feasts in towns like Lagos, Albufeira, and Tavira, where restaurants serve grilled fish, **cataplana** (seafood stew), and **sardinhas assadas** (grilled sardines).

Local Highlights: Take a boat tour to discover secluded coves and caves, where you can fish or snorkel. Many tours include stops at local seafood restaurants, allowing you to savor freshly caught dishes right by the water.

Spain and Portugal offer a wealth of culinary experiences that celebrate their rich food cultures. From the vibrant atmosphere of tapas tours to the exquisite wines of La Rioja and Douro Valley, and the mouthwatering seafood of Galicia and the Algarve, food enthusiasts will find a treasure trove of flavors and experiences. Embrace the diverse culinary heritage of the Iberian Peninsula and indulge in unforgettable dining experiences that reflect the region's rich traditions and local ingredients.

Markets and Local Food Experiences

Exploring the local markets in Spain and Portugal offers an authentic glimpse into the culinary culture of these vibrant countries. Markets are not just places to shop; they are social hubs where locals gather, and visitors can immerse themselves in the sights, sounds, and flavors of the region. Here's a comprehensive overview of some of the most iconic markets and local food experiences you can enjoy in Spain and Portugal.

Spain

La Boqueria in Barcelona:

Overview: Located just off the bustling La Rambla, La Boqueria is one of Barcelona's most famous markets, attracting both locals and tourists. With its vibrant stalls and colorful displays, it is a feast for the senses.

Fresh Produce: The market is renowned for its fresh fruits and vegetables, including exotic and seasonal varieties. Vendors often provide samples, making it easy to discover new flavors.

Cured Meats and Cheeses: La Boqueria is home to numerous stalls selling cured meats, such as **jamón ibérico** (Iberian ham) and a variety of cheeses from different regions of Spain.

Seafood: Fresh seafood is abundant, with stalls offering everything from octopus and prawns to shellfish and local fish. Many vendors also sell prepared seafood dishes for a quick snack.

Tapas and Ready-to-Eat Dishes: Enjoy a meal at one of the small bars or stalls serving tapas, such as **patatas bravas**, **croquetas**, and **churros** with chocolate. A must-try is the freshly prepared **seafood paella** or the famous **Spanish omelet**.

Local Experience: Join a guided food tour of La Boqueria to learn about the history of the market, meet local vendors, and taste various traditional dishes. It's an excellent way to explore the culinary diversity of Barcelona.

Mercado de San Miguel in Madrid:

Overview: This historic market, located near the Plaza Mayor, has transformed into a culinary hotspot featuring gourmet food stalls and tapas bars. The market's elegant architecture and lively atmosphere make it a must-visit.

Gourmet Delicacies: Mercado de San Miguel boasts a wide variety of gourmet products, including artisanal cheeses, cured meats, olives, and gourmet chocolates. Each stall showcases the best of Spanish culinary traditions.

Tapas and Small Plates: Experience an array of tapas, from traditional favorites to innovative dishes. Popular options include **grilled octopus, anchovies**, and **mini-burgers**.

Wine and Cider: Many stalls offer wine tastings, showcasing the best of Spanish wines, including **Rioja, Albariño**, and local ciders from Asturias. You can also find a selection of craft beers and vermouth.

Local Experience: Participate in a cooking class or wine pairing workshop held at the market to deepen your appreciation of Spanish cuisine. This interactive experience allows you to learn from local chefs and enjoy a delicious meal.

Portugal

Time Out Market in Lisbon:

Overview: Housed in the historic Mercado da Ribeira, the Time Out Market is a modern food hall that brings together some of the best culinary talents in Lisbon under one roof. It offers a diverse range of food options from traditional Portuguese dishes to international cuisine.

Culinary Variety: The market features stalls run by top chefs and renowned restaurants, offering everything from **bacalhau à Brás** (codfish) to gourmet burgers and sushi.

Local Specialties: Don't miss out on trying **pastéis de nata** (custard tarts) from the famous **Manteigaria** stall, or sample **petiscos** (Portuguese tapas) from local vendors.

Craft Beverages: The market also boasts an impressive selection of wines, craft beers, and cocktails, allowing visitors to pair their meals with the perfect drink.

Local Experience: Attend food demonstrations or chef-led workshops hosted at the market to learn more about Portuguese culinary traditions and techniques.

Bolhão Market in Porto:

Overview: Bolhão Market is a traditional market that embodies the charm of Porto. With its lively atmosphere and array of local products, it's a great place to experience the city's culinary culture.

Fresh Produce: The market is known for its vibrant stalls filled with fresh fruits, vegetables, herbs, and flowers. Local vendors offer seasonal produce, allowing visitors to taste the flavors of the region.

Seafood and Fish: As a coastal city, Porto's market features an impressive selection of fresh seafood. Stalls sell everything from sardines and clams to octopus and crabs, reflecting the region's maritime heritage.

Cured Meats and Cheese: Explore the stalls offering local cheeses, **salami**, and **chouriço** (smoked sausage). Many vendors also provide samples, making it easy to discover your favorites.

Local Experience: Visit Bolhão Market in the morning to witness the hustle and bustle of local vendors and shoppers. Consider taking a cooking class nearby to learn how to prepare traditional dishes using ingredients sourced from the market.

Exploring the markets of Spain and Portugal provides a unique culinary experience that highlights the region's rich food culture. From the vibrant stalls of La Boqueria and Mercado de San Miguel to the gourmet offerings at Time Out Market and the traditional charm of Bolhão Market, these markets invite visitors to immerse themselves in the local flavors and culinary traditions. Whether you're sampling tapas, indulging in seafood, or savoring wines, each market offers a memorable experience that reflects the heart and soul of its respective culture.

CHAPTER 9

Sustainability and Responsible Travel

Traveling sustainably in Spain and Portugal is becoming increasingly important as awareness of environmental impacts grows. Both countries offer a wealth of natural beauty, rich cultural heritage, and local communities that thrive on tourism. By adopting responsible travel practices, visitors can enjoy their experiences while minimizing their footprint and supporting the preservation of these vibrant destinations. Here's a comprehensive guide on how to travel sustainably in Spain and Portugal.

How to Travel Sustainably in Spain and Portugal

Be Mindful of Your Waste:

Reduce Single-Use Plastics: Bring a reusable water bottle to refill throughout your trip, minimizing reliance on single-use plastic bottles. Many cities in Spain and Portugal have drinking fountains or public water access points.

Carry Reusable Bags: Use reusable shopping bags when visiting markets or stores. This practice helps reduce plastic waste and is often required in many establishments.

Practice Leave No Trace: Always dispose of your waste properly and avoid littering in natural areas. Take your trash with you if no bins are available.

Choose Sustainable Activities:

Support Wildlife Conservation: Participate in eco-tours that focus on wildlife conservation and education. Look for tours that prioritize responsible viewing practices and support local conservation efforts.

Respect Natural Areas: When hiking or exploring natural parks, stay on designated paths, avoid disturbing wildlife, and follow local guidelines to protect fragile ecosystems.

Educate Yourself:

Learn Local Customs: Understanding and respecting local customs, traditions, and cultural sensitivities can enhance your travel experience and promote positive interactions with locals.

Choose Responsible Tour Operators: Research and select tour companies that have sustainable practices, such as minimizing environmental impact, supporting local communities, and promoting cultural heritage.

Eco-Friendly Hotels and Green Tourism Initiatives

Sustainable Accommodation Options:

Eco-Friendly Hotels: Many hotels in Spain and Portugal are adopting eco-friendly practices, such as energy-efficient systems, water conservation methods, and using sustainable materials. Look for hotels with certifications like Green Key or EarthCheck, which recognize environmental responsibility.

Rural Tourism: Consider staying in rural guesthouses or agriturismos that promote sustainable tourism practices. These accommodations often focus on organic farming, local produce, and community involvement.

Green Tourism Initiatives:

Conservation Programs: Participate in programs that focus on environmental conservation and education. Many national parks and nature reserves offer volunteer opportunities for visitors to engage in conservation efforts.

Community Projects: Some regions have initiatives to support local crafts and traditional practices. Look for experiences that allow you to learn about local artisans and contribute to their livelihoods.

Supporting Local Businesses and Communities

- **Eat Local**:

Farm-to-Table Dining: Dine at restaurants that prioritize local ingredients, supporting regional farmers and producers. Look for menus that highlight seasonal dishes and traditional recipes.

Markets and Street Vendors: Visit local markets and street food vendors to sample authentic dishes. This approach not only supports local economies but also provides a genuine taste of the culture.

Shop Local:

Artisans and Craftspeople: Purchase souvenirs directly from local artisans to ensure that your money supports the community. Seek out unique, handcrafted items rather than mass-produced goods.

Fair Trade Products: When shopping, look for fair trade certified products, ensuring that producers receive a fair wage for their work.

- **Engage with the Community**:

Cultural Exchanges: Participate in cultural exchange programs, workshops, or homestays that connect you with locals. This immersive experience fosters understanding and respect for the community and its traditions.

Reducing Your Carbon Footprin

- **Utilize Public Transportation**:

Trains and Buses: Spain and Portugal have extensive public transport networks. Opt for trains and buses instead of renting a car for long distances, as this reduces emissions and offers a chance to relax while enjoying scenic views.

Metro and Trams: In major cities like Madrid, Barcelona, Lisbon, and Porto, utilize metro systems and trams for efficient and eco-friendly transportation.

Bike Rentals and Walking:

Bike Rentals: Many cities have bike-sharing programs or rental shops. Cycling is a fantastic way to explore urban areas while minimizing your carbon footprint. Look for dedicated bike lanes and paths for safe riding.

Walking Tours: Explore cities on foot to immerse yourself in the local culture and architecture. Walking reduces emissions and provides a deeper connection to the surroundings.

Carbon Offset Programs:

Offset Your Travel: Consider participating in carbon offset programs that allow you to invest in environmental projects to compensate for your travel emissions. Many organizations focus on reforestation, renewable energy, and conservation efforts.

Traveling sustainably in Spain and Portugal not only enhances your experience but also contributes to the preservation of the environment and local cultures. By making mindful choices, supporting local businesses, and embracing eco-friendly practices, you can ensure that your travels have a positive impact on these beautiful destinations. Engage with the communities you visit, appreciate the local heritage, and leave a

lasting impression that promotes sustainability for
future travelers.

CHAPTER 10

Health and Safety

When traveling in Spain and Portugal, it's essential to prioritize your health and safety to ensure a smooth and enjoyable experience. From understanding local laws to knowing how to access healthcare services, being informed can help you navigate potential challenges. Here's a comprehensive overview of health and safety considerations for your trip.

Staying Safe

General Travel Safety:

Stay Aware of Your Surroundings: Like any major tourist destinations, some areas in Spain and Portugal may have higher crime rates. Stay alert, especially in crowded places such as markets, public transport, and tourist attractions.

Keep Valuables Secure: Use a money belt or anti-theft backpack to keep your passport, money, and valuables safe. Avoid carrying large amounts of cash and only bring what you need for the day.

Know Your Accommodation's Location: Familiarize yourself with your surroundings and the location of your accommodation. Ensure you have a plan for getting back safely after a night out.

1. **Avoiding Scams**:

Common Scams: Be cautious of common scams such as fake charity collectors, overly friendly strangers offering unsolicited help, and distraction scams where one person diverts your attention while another steals your belongings.

Use Reputable Services: When booking tours, transportation, or accommodations, use trusted platforms and read reviews. Avoid deals that seem too good to be true.

2. **Local Laws**:

Respect Local Laws and Customs: Familiarize yourself with local laws, customs, and cultural norms. For example, public drunkenness is frowned upon, and some cities have strict laws about littering and smoking.

Drug Laws: Spain and Portugal have strict drug laws. While some substances may be decriminalized, possession and use can still result in fines or legal issues. Always adhere to the laws regarding alcohol consumption, especially in public spaces.

Health Care Information

- **Healthcare System**:

Public Healthcare: Spain and Portugal have public healthcare systems that provide quality medical services. EU citizens can use their European Health Insurance Card (EHIC) for access to public healthcare services. Non-EU travelers should ensure they have adequate travel insurance to cover medical expenses.

Private Healthcare: Private healthcare facilities are widely available and often offer shorter waiting times and English-speaking staff. However, services may require upfront payment.

- **Pharmacies**:

Finding Pharmacies: Pharmacies (farmacias in Spanish and farmácias in Portuguese) are easily found in cities and towns. They display a green cross (Spain) or a blue cross (Portugal) outside.

Prescription and Over-the-Counter Medications: Many common medications are available over-the-counter. For prescription medications, bring a copy of your prescription and check the legality of specific drugs in the country.

Emergency Numbers and Contact Information

1. **Emergency Services**:
   - **General Emergency Number**: Dial **112** for emergency assistance (police, fire, ambulance) in both Spain and Portugal.
   - **Local Hospital Contact**: Research the nearest hospitals or clinics in advance and note their contact information in case of emergencies.
2. **Consulate and Embassy Information**:
   - **Locate Your Country's Embassy or Consulate**: Familiarize yourself with the contact information of your country's embassy or consulate in Spain and Portugal. They can provide assistance in case of lost passports or legal issues.

Travel Insurance

Why You Need Travel Insurance:

Protection Against Unexpected Events: Travel insurance offers protection against unforeseen circumstances, such as trip cancellations, medical emergencies, lost luggage, and travel delays.

Peace of Mind: Having insurance can provide peace of mind, allowing you to enjoy your trip without worrying about potential financial burdens.

What to Look For:

Comprehensive Coverage: Ensure your policy includes coverage for medical emergencies, trip cancellations, lost or stolen belongings, and personal liability.

24/7 Assistance: Look for a plan that offers 24/7 emergency assistance, allowing you to get help no matter the time or situation.

Pre-existing Conditions: If you have pre-existing medical conditions, check if they are covered under the policy. Some insurers offer specific coverage for these conditions.

Adventure Activities: If you plan to engage in adventure activities like hiking, skiing, or scuba diving, ensure your policy covers these activities as many standard plans may exclude them.

By prioritizing health and safety during your travels in Spain and Portugal, you can enjoy a worry-free experience. Stay informed about local laws, take precautions to avoid scams, and have a plan for healthcare access. Additionally, investing in comprehensive travel insurance will provide added security, allowing you to explore these beautiful countries with peace of mind.

CHAPTER 11

Practical Tips

Navigating Spain and Portugal can be a delightful experience, but knowing some practical tips can make your trip smoother and more enjoyable. From understanding tipping customs to connecting with locals, here's a comprehensive guide to help you travel with confidence.

Tipping Culture in Spain and Portugal

General Tipping Practices:

Spain: Tipping is appreciated but not mandatory. In restaurants, it's common to leave small change or round up the bill, typically adding around 5-10% for excellent service. In bars, leaving the small coins or rounding up is also customary, especially if you've ordered food.

Portugal: Similar to Spain, tipping in Portugal is not compulsory, but it is welcomed. A tip of 5-10% is common in restaurants if the service is good. For cafes and bars, rounding up the bill or leaving small coins is appreciated.

Other Situations:

Taxis: In both countries, rounding up the fare is standard practice, but you can add more if the driver was especially helpful.

Hotels: Consider tipping porters €1-2 per bag and leaving a few coins for housekeeping if you are staying for several nights.

Electricity, Wi-Fi, and SIM Cards

Electricity:

Voltage and Plugs: Both Spain and Portugal use a standard voltage of 230V and the frequency of 50Hz. The plug types are European two-pin (Type C and Type F). It's advisable to carry a universal adapter to charge your devices.

Wi-Fi:

Availability: Wi-Fi is widely available in hotels, cafés, and public places. Many restaurants and bars offer free Wi-Fi to customers. However, in rural areas, connectivity may be less reliable.

Cafés and Public Spaces: Look for signs indicating free Wi-Fi. Just be cautious about using public Wi-Fi for sensitive transactions; using a VPN is a good practice for added security.

SIM Cards:

Buying a SIM Card: If you plan to stay longer or need consistent data access, consider purchasing a local SIM card. Major providers in Spain include Movistar, Vodafone, and Orange, while in Portugal, MEO, NOS, and Vodafone are popular.

Prepaid Options: Prepaid SIM cards are available at airports, convenience stores, and mobile phone shops. They typically come with various data packages to suit your needs. Be sure to bring your passport, as it may be required for purchase.

Local Etiquette

Do's:

Do Greet People: A friendly greeting goes a long way. In Spain, it's common to greet with "Hola" (Hello) or "Buenos días" (Good morning), while in Portugal, you can say "Olá" or "Bom dia." A handshake is typical; close friends may greet with a kiss on both cheeks.

Do Try the Local Cuisine: Embrace the local food culture. Ask locals for recommendations on where to eat, and don't hesitate to try new dishes.

Do Be Punctual: While it's common for locals to be a bit more relaxed about time, being punctual for business or formal engagements is appreciated.

Don'ts:

Don't Discuss Politics or Religion: These topics can be sensitive, especially in casual conversations. It's best to avoid them unless you know the person well.

Don't Rush Meals: Dining is often seen as a leisurely activity in both countries. Take your time to enjoy meals, and don't expect quick service; it's part of the culture.

Don't Assume English is Widely Spoken: While many people, especially in tourist areas, speak English, not everyone does. Learning a few basic phrases in Spanish or Portuguese can be very helpful and appreciated by locals.

Public Holidays and Festivals to Be Aware Of

Public Holidays:

Spain: Key public holidays include:

New Year's Day (Año Nuevo) - January 1

- **Epiphany (Día de Reyes)** - January 6
- **National Day (Fiesta Nacional)** - October 12
- **Christmas (Navidad)** - December 25

o **Portugal**: Major public holidays include:
- **New Year's Day (Ano Novo)** - January 1
- **Carnival (Carnaval)** - Date varies (February/March)
- **Portugal Day (Dia de Portugal)** - June 10
- **Christmas (Natal)** - December 25

2. **Festivals**:
   o **Spain**:

- **La Tomatina** (Buñol, August): A massive tomato-throwing festival that attracts tourists worldwide.
- **Feria de Abril** (Seville, April): A vibrant festival featuring flamenco, traditional dress, and local food.
  - **Portugal**:
    - **Festa de São João** (Porto, June 23-24): A lively celebration with fireworks, music, and traditional street festivities.
    - **Festa de Santo António** (Lisbon, June 12-13): Known for its street parties, grilled sardines, and lively atmosphere.

By keeping these practical tips in mind, you can navigate your travels in Spain and Portugal more effectively. Embracing local customs, understanding the culture, and being prepared for different situations will enhance your experience and help you connect with the vibrant societies of these two beautiful countries.

CHAPTER 12

Author's Recommendations

Traveling through Spain and Portugal can be an exhilarating experience filled with rich culture, stunning landscapes, and delicious cuisine. To help you make the most of your journey, here are my insider tips for exploring these beautiful countries like a local, along with some hidden gems and personal favorites that will enhance your adventure.

Insider Tips for Exploring Spain and Portugal Like a Local

Embrace the Siesta:

In many parts of Spain and some areas of Portugal, the afternoon siesta is a cherished tradition. Shops and businesses may close between 2 PM and 5 PM, allowing locals to relax and recharge. Use this time to enjoy a leisurely lunch, read a book, or take a nap to rejuvenate for the evening ahead.

Eat at the Right Time:

Dinner in Spain typically starts around 9 PM, while in Portugal, it's usually around 8 PM. Adjust your meal times accordingly to fully enjoy the dining experience. Don't miss out on traditional tapas in Spain or petiscos in Portugal, which are perfect for sampling various dishes.

- **Engage with Locals**:

Making an effort to speak a few words of Spanish or Portuguese can go a long way in connecting with locals. Most people appreciate the attempt and will be happy to help you with recommendations or directions.

- **Utilize Public Transport**:

Both Spain and Portugal have excellent public transport systems, including metro, buses, and trains. They are often the most efficient and economical way to get around. Consider purchasing multi-day passes for unlimited travel.

- **Attend Local Events and Festivals**:

Check local calendars for festivals and events happening during your visit. Participating in these celebrations offers a unique glimpse into the culture and traditions of each region.

Hidden Gems Off the Beaten Path

Spain:

Ronda: This stunning town in Andalusia is known for its dramatic cliffside location and picturesque bridge, Puente Nuevo. Explore its charming old town and enjoy breathtaking views of the surrounding countryside.

Cádiz: Located on the southwestern coast, this ancient port city boasts beautiful beaches, a vibrant atmosphere, and delicious seafood. Stroll through its historic streets and visit the local markets.

Portugal:

Évora: A UNESCO World Heritage site in the Alentejo region, Évora is known for its well-preserved Roman Temple and charming medieval streets. It offers a quieter, more authentic Portuguese experience.

Tavira: This charming coastal town in the Algarve features stunning architecture, beautiful beaches, and a relaxed atmosphere. Don't miss the picturesque Roman bridge and the local seafood restaurants.

Personal Favorites: Restaurants, Cafes, and Scenic Spots

- **Restaurants**:

Spain:

Bodega 1900 (Barcelona): A modern take on a classic vermuteria, this restaurant offers a fantastic selection of tapas and vermouth. The ambiance is lively and perfect for a fun night out.

Casa Lucio (Madrid): Famous for its delicious huevos rotos (broken eggs) and traditional Spanish cuisine, this restaurant is a must-visit for an authentic Madrid dining experience.

Portugal:

Taberna da Rua das Flores (Lisbon): This intimate eatery serves contemporary Portuguese dishes made from fresh, local ingredients. Reservations are recommended due to its popularity.

Cantinho do Avillez (Porto): Celebrity chef José Avillez's restaurant offers a modern twist on traditional Portuguese dishes in a cozy setting.

Cafés:

Spain:

Chocolatería San Ginés (Madrid): Known for its churros and thick hot chocolate, this historic café is perfect for an afternoon treat or a late-night snack.

Café de Oriente (Madrid): With stunning views of the Royal Palace, this café is a great spot for coffee or a light meal in a beautiful setting.

Portugal:

A Brasileira (Lisbon): A historic café where you can enjoy a bica (espresso) and soak in the vibrant atmosphere. It's famous for its association with Portuguese poets and artists.

Pastéis de Belém (Lisbon): This iconic bakery is renowned for its pastéis de nata (custard tarts). Be prepared for a line, but the delicious treats are worth the wait.

Scenic Spots:

Spain:

Park Güell (Barcelona): Designed by Antoni Gaudí, this colorful park offers whimsical architecture and stunning views of the city. It's a perfect spot for a leisurely stroll.

Mirador de San Nicolás (Granada): This viewpoint offers breathtaking views of the Alhambra against the backdrop of the Sierra Nevada mountains, especially at sunset.

Portugal:

Pena Palace (Sintra): This vibrant, fairy-tale palace is set on a hilltop and offers spectacular views of the surrounding landscape. Don't miss exploring the enchanting gardens.

Cape Roca: The westernmost point of mainland Europe, Cape Roca features dramatic cliffs and stunning ocean views. It's a perfect spot for nature lovers and photographers.

With these insider tips, hidden gems, and personal favorites, you'll be well-equipped to explore Spain and Portugal like a local. Embrace the culture, savor the cuisine, and discover the enchanting beauty that these countries have to offer. Happy travels!

CONCLUSION

As we conclude this travel guide to Spain and Portugal, it's essential to reflect on the vibrant tapestry of experiences that await you in these two remarkable countries. Each destination, from the sun-drenched beaches of the Algarve to the bustling streets of Madrid, offers a unique blend of history, culture, and natural beauty that captivates travelers from around the globe.

Throughout this guide, we've explored the must-visit cities and hidden gems, delving into the rich cultural traditions that define Spanish and Portuguese life. From savoring exquisite tapas in Seville to indulging in the sweetness of pastéis de nata in Lisbon, each culinary experience is a window into the heart and soul of these nations. The warm hospitality of the locals, the lively festivals, and the mesmerizing landscapes all contribute to the unforgettable memories you'll create during your journey.

As you embark on your adventure, remember to embrace the local customs, savor the diverse cuisines, and take time to connect with the people you meet along the way. Whether you're wandering through the historic streets of Porto, marveling at the architectural wonders of Barcelona, or soaking in the sun on the beaches of Costa del Sol, allow yourself to be immersed in the vibrant cultures and traditions that make Spain and Portugal so special.

We hope this guide serves as a valuable resource, providing you with the practical tips, insights, and inspiration needed to explore these beautiful countries with confidence. As you pack your bags and set off on your journey, remember that the adventure is just beginning. Spain and Portugal are waiting to share their stories, landscapes, and flavors with you. Safe travels, and may your journey be filled with exploration, discovery, and joy!

Made in United States
Troutdale, OR
12/21/2024

27172440R00106